WELCOME

TO

My Mother's Legacy

By

Laura I-dell

Scriptor House LLC

2810 N Church St Wilmington, Delaware, 19802

www.scriptorhouse.com

Phone: +1302-205-2043

Published by Scriptor House LLC

Paperback ISBN: 979-8-88692-248-6

eBook ISBN: 979-8-88692-249-3

Hardback ISBN: 979-8-88692-295-0

Because of the dynamic nature of the Internet, any web addresses or links contained in this book may have changed since publication and may no longer be valid. The opinions expressed in this manuscript are solely the opinions of the author and do not represent the opinions or thoughts of the publisher and the publisher hereby disclaims any responsibility for them. The author has represented and warranted full ownership and/or legal right to publish all the materials in this book.

The Fruit of the Womb
Volume 1

was given

TO

____

FROM

____

ON

____

OCCASION

____

AUTHOR

____

Acknowledgement

While I am indeed grateful to my family members,

And friends, as well as colleagues, and others, who believed in me,

And encouraged me, as I wrote 'The Fruit of the Womb,' I am so

Much more grateful to God. The One, who, notwithstanding

His sovereignty, His supremacy, His holiness, took

The time to acknowledge you and me, through

Christ Jesus "His only begotten Son".

For that reason, "I proclaim the name of the LORD:

Ascribe greatness to our God" (Deuteronomy 32:3),

Through Christ Jesus our Lord. For "he who acknowledges

The Son has the Father also." (1 John 2:23)

The Foundation

"*A*ll Scripture is given by inspiration of God,
And is profitable for doctrine, for reproof, for correction,
For instruction in righteousness, that the man of God
May be complete, thoroughly equipped for every
Good work." (2 Timothy 3:16–17)

So, regardless of how we might live our lives;
Or stray from the Word of God, our manual in life is
Still the Holy Bible, but, when it comes to the Holy Bible,
"Do you understand what you are reading?" (Acts 8:26–40)

For this purpose: In 'The Fruit of the Womb,'
A wealth of Scriptures has been applied, to guide us in life.
And so, as you read about 'The Life of My Mother', you will
also be reading about "Life in Christ". (Romans 8:1–11)

About the Author

The author was born on the 26th day of July, in one of the most beautiful and loved countries in the world; The Bahamas. A vacation destination for travelers from all walks of life, due to its many islands that are alive and rich in culture; that have their remarkable prehistoric sites, breathtaking beaches and product.

This author has had an aspiration for writing since youth, and today, her writings have become her personal ministry. Wherein, it gives her a divine opportunity to spread the Word of God, not only through her mother's life's journey but also her journey, as a daughter.

And so, by way of her writings, she is going about in her hometown, and other parts of the world, where her feet, perhaps, may never tread, spreading "the Gospel of our Lord Jesus Christ" (2 Thessalonians 1:8–12). She said, 'she knows her writings are not perfect; maybe, they contain many errors, but if God, whose way of writing is beyond perfection (Exodus 24:12, 31:18), wants to use her, even in her imperfection, then, she rejoice in being of service to God.'

So that you, beloved reader, would have knowledge of; the sequel to 'The Fruit of the Womb, Volume 1 (My Mother's Legacy)' is 'The Fruit of the Womb, Volume 2 (My Legacy)', wherein, the author shares her life, as a wife, and a mother.

You may wish to follow.

What is one of the things that kindle this writer's heart?

You already know it is writing!

And to support her writings, to make them authentic, and effective, she gathers her most important materials from the Holy Bible.

One of her favorite pieces can be found in John 1:43–51, which reads: "Now Philip was from Bethsaida, the city of Andrew and Peter.

Philip found Nathanael and said to him, "We have found Him of whom Moses in the law, and also the prophets, wrote–Jesus of Nazareth, the son of Joseph."

And Nathanael said to him, "Can anything good come out of Nazareth?"

Philip said to him, "Come and see."

Today, I ask you; *can anything good come out of* the first generation of the mother, whom this legacy represents? Since many saw her children, as nothing.

Yes! An author did!

And while The Bahamas, and the rest of the world, are just getting to know about this young innovative writer, well, not in age, but in spirit, she is already well-known to God.

The God, whom I believe, will make every step of her journey as a Christian author satisfying, successful, profitable, and rewarding, because rather than take the fleeting path, she took the path that leads to "eternal life in Christ Jesus our Lord." (Romans 6:20 23)

My Mother's Table

Chapter 1
My Mother's Legacy

Chapter 2
Words of Life

Chapter 3
Grateful Hearts

Chapter 4
The Conclusion

Chapter 1

My Mother's Legacy

"*C*an a woman forget her nursing child,
And not have compassion on the son of her womb?
Surely they may forget, yet I will not forget you.
See, I have inscribed you on the palms of
My hands; your walls are continually
Before Me." *(Isaiah 49:15–16)*

Introduction

*T*hrough this legacy, you will come to know all about a woman, a single mother, a wife, a widow, whom God moved mightily in the life of; an individual who, through the power of God, has proven once you are in Christ, no matter what weakens you, you still have "strength… made perfect in weakness." (2 Corinthians 12:9–10)

As you journey through *my mother's legacy*, my prayer is that it will be a blessing to your heart, your soul, and mind, as taking long walks in the garden of Scriptures has been, and is to mine; that it will impact your life, positively, as an individual.

My sincere hope is that *my mother's legacy* will guide a young woman to "looking unto Jesus, the author and finisher of our faith" (Hebrews 12:2), of our lives, for help, and not to man, nor the world.

May this legacy bring to the mind of a wife, that the One (Isaiah 54:5), who is in heaven, also requires her devotion, and not be devoted to only her earthly husband.

I trust that *my mother's legacy* will give a single mother, godly courage, and the will, to never give up on God, no matter what she might fall short of in her home, and that includes a man.

For if we live daily, by faith in God, "without wavering", and "with no doubting", at night, we can "both lie down in peace, and sleep", and when morning comes, God will wake us up laughing to the desires of our heart. And our laughter will go on way longer than any of our nights ever was, because God has blessed us to "see the goodness of the LORD in the land of the living." (Psalm 27:13)

Good morning, Mother, I believe you have had a peaceful night.

As you continue to journey through *my mother's legacy,* may it also take you to a path where you will, unfailingly lay-up prayers in heaven (Revelation 8:1-4), not only for your child, or your children, but also for yourself. And in return, may God send down His blessings upon you and His wisdom to be displayed inside, and outside your home for all to see.

And may you, in your journey; "Watch, stand fast in the faith, be brave, be strong" (1 Corinthians 16:13–14), always.

"Now may the God of hope fill you with all joy and peace in believing, that you may abound in hope by the power of the Holy Spirit." (Romans 15:13)

Heavenly Father, I ask this of You; let this mother, and "all those rejoice who put their trust in You; let them ever shout for joy, because You defend them; let those also who love Your name be joyful in You.

For You, O LORD, will bless the righteous; with favor You will surround him as with a shield." (Psalm 5:11–12)

Father, thank You for Your boundless blessings and for Your wonderful works toward us. In Jesus' mighty name. Amen and Amen.

Footnotes:

Genesis 2:22, Psalms 139:14, 121:1–2, 146:3–5,

30:4–6, 126:1–3, 37:4, 4:8, 138:8, 1 John 2:15–17,

Hebrews 10:23, James 1:6, Isaiah 26:3, Lamentations 3:22–26,

2 Corinthians 12:14, Matthew 18:18, Proverbs 31:25–27

The Interview

*F*ollowing the interview, I could not conclude, if I should still write about the legacy of this woman, for the sole purpose of not wanting to offend, or bring discomfort to anybody; above all, to her beloved children, and other dear family members. But, Revelation 21:5 incited me with this one word; "write"! And so through the direction of the Holy Spirit, I have written.

However, not every aspect of this woman's life was recorded. The early and latter parts, mainly, have been abridged. Because, if I were to recount every event of this woman's life, they would be chronicled in a number of books, not on a number of pages, which narrate love, wisdom, hope, strength, trust, faith, thoughtfulness, togetherness, resolution, reconciliation, amusement, audaciousness, and appeal.

And sadly, these sheets also speak of division, and of much pain and sorrow in the life of a woman, whom I have learned was one of the most beautiful women on the island on which she was born.

In wanting to know more about the life of the woman, who greatly inspired my life; as a journalist, I then sought after an interview with one of her elder daughters, who freely shared with me, a whole lot more than I had expected to be fed. And one of the things among the many that she mentioned in our heart-to-heart, and stayed with me is 'Others said her mother used her beauty to her advantage.'

And what is wrong with that?

Did they ask her to enter a Beauty Pageant for the love of her country, and she refused to? I asked her.

No. She replied.

In the interview, I also learned that because of the way her mother's husband died, which was her father, not only did outsiders, but family members as well, looked down upon her mother, and her children and labeled them.

Now, rather than her mother picking up the broken pieces of her life, and asking God to rebuild it, so that her, and her children could have a new start in life; her mother, perpetually made, not just mistakes. She made one bad choice after another, causing herself to be despised even more, by others, and to the point of where her children were called ill-names, continuously.

As I digested some of the names she and her siblings were called; as I was listening to the many cheerless accounts of this woman's life being unveiled by her daughter, whom I am sure, remembers more than she cares to, my own emotions were also uncovered right before her.

After the interview; with a sorrowful heart, I asked myself, 'What if this mother did have a blueprint, with high hopes for herself, and her children, but because she shared not only herself, but also her family plan with the wrong man, or men, after the death of her husband, they got crushed, and so did her willpower (Proverbs 17:22)?'

So, if this mother did not look to God, to help her fulfill her family plans, but to man, who only wanted to have a good time, and then, move on, how could she have taught her children anything different from what she had taught them?

If this mother, after the death of her husband, had yet, to meet the Man who was right for her; the Man who did not want to have a good time, and then, move on, but remain in her life, and in her children's lives forever, for God Himself is love everlasting, how could she have shown her children anything different from what she had shown them?

Yet, the many things I have heard about this woman, as a wife cannot be compared to the courage she has had as a mother, nor to the faith she had built in her God, her Lord and Savior.

And that is the inspiration I will carry with me for the rest of my life because, not only will it help me to be a better mother to my children; it will also aid me to be a more courageous and upstanding journalist.

This woman's life story "has shown you, O man, what is good; and what does the LORD require of you but to do justly, to love mercy, and to walk humbly with your God?" (Micah 6:8)

So, today, as you learn about the histories of a woman, a single mother, a wife, a widow, whom God moved mightily in the life of; will also come to believe that once you are in Christ, no matter what weakens you, you still have "strength… made perfect in weakness." (2 Corinthians 12:9–10)

The Life of My Mother

*M*y mother was the youngest of five children; and although she was born in a Christian home, with both parents; she still became a single mother, and experienced the adversities of life, at a very young age.

And my mother, despite there being generational properties, where she could have very well inherited her portion, and built a house on it; hoping to make a better life for herself, and her younger children, moved from the island on which she was born, to the capital.

Of course, in the capital, there are many more opportunities, and perhaps, better ones. But, no mother can see what conditions come with some of those opportunities. Not until it is too late.

After having lived in the capital for some time, many who got to know her began calling her mother, either through the affection they felt for her or were simply following the pattern of her biological children.

Ironically, except for one; even her grandchildren and great-grandchildren called her mother, while for some unknown reason, her two youngest children called her *mommy*. Also, out of all the children, they were the only two born in the capital.

How my youngest sibling and I did not model *mother*, like the rest of her children, and were the only two born in the capital, I am still trying to figure that out. Even the way we knew our mother was quite different from the way our elder siblings knew her.

And I said that based on what we heard from them, and according to what our mother, herself, told us, about her earlier years in life.

While my mother did not guide my siblings and me by the wisdom of God only by what she thought was best for us; some of those same things she taught us, I later found, were written in the Scriptures.

And although we attended school, our mother did not rear us in our schooling, the way a parent is supposed to.

As for church, she took us regularly, but, as opposed to living fully by the Word of God, somewhere along the way, she would throw in a philosophy of her own

You know, one of the things that I find very hard to comprehend, as it relates to the philosophy of single mothers is some, without a doubt, believe they are both father and mother in their child's life, or their children's lives, and have to work twice as hard, in raising and supporting them.

For me, the truth is, no woman has both male and female sex cells and when they come in contact with each other, she gets herself pregnant.

So, no matter how hard any woman, who is a single mother, has to work, even if it's triply hard, she can never, ever be the father, in her child's life, or her children's lives.

Besides, whether the father is deceased, or is alive but is not around, there is one Man, who never forsakes His fatherly role.

All she has to do is make room in her life, and in her home, for Him, and He will be the best Father there is, and not only to her child or her children, but also to her.

A single mother, in knowing who her heavenly Father is, when she sees a curveball heading in her direction, will not stand there, and watch it spiral into her life. She will remember that "He gives power to the weak, and those who have no might He increases strength" (Isaiah 40:29), and will knock that ball right back to wherever it came from (Philippians 4:13).

If she does not, when it strikes her, her child, or her children whom she loves dearly, will feel the impact of it, as well.

Remember, Mother, "God has dealt to each one a measure of faith" (Romans 12:3). So you "always ought to pray and not lose heart" (Luke 18:1), for "if you faint in the day of adversity, your strength is small" (Proverbs 24:10).

Now although my mother did what she thought was best for her children, and not what was right for them, still, when others look at her picture, and to them, it says only a thousand words or less, or perhaps, no words at all; my youngest sibling and I can see books, upon books.

And this very book tells about how our mother became independent of men and solely dependent on God.

The eras of my mother, in addition to what I know, were of distinction, audaciousness, amusement, and sadly, of much sorrow.

And while she was one of the most beautiful women on the island, where she was born, my youngest sibling and I were told she used her beauty to her advantage.

In all the years of knowing my mother, I have never seen her wear makeup. She did not have to, she was a very pretty woman, naturally, and she always looked radiant.

Now, if she was this beautiful, and attractive in her older years, then, how much more stunning was she, in her younger years?

The key question is: How did my mother use her beauty to her advantage? One would think that they asked her to enter a beauty pageant, to save her whole country, but she refused to, to save only herself.

My mother made choices that caused many people, including her family members, to look down on her, and to talk badly about her, to the point where they wanted nothing to do with her, or her children. And just as this went on for years, the effects of this lasted for years and impacted the lives of her children. And while the weight of it rested more heavily on some of her children, than it did on the others, it was painful for all.

Did my mother love her children enough to recognize what was happening to them?

Did she even care enough for her children, to have sought a way to remedy the situation, so that she and her children could live better lives?

The thing is, when my mother started having children, she still, many times acted as if she had no children.

That could mean she loved and cared only about herself.

Maybe, my mother did not realize what kind of life she had lived, until after she stopped having children.

My mother was employed as a domestic worker for many years, and in certain jobs she went on, be it to strangers, or family members, I felt, she accepted far too much of the worse from her employers, for the salary they were paying her, or not paying her (Deuteronomy 24:14–15).

Even though my youngest sibling and I were the only ones born in the capital, as little girls, we still got to spend a lot of time on the island.

And I can recall us, watching our mother, daily, for years, cutting sisal, and scraping it; breaking tops, and leaving them out in the sun to dry, and then later, stripped them. With these items, she produced rolls of plait and weaved many baskets. And we were always excited to see our mother's finished work which for each time was outstanding.

My mother, at that time, was self-employed, and her business place was a bench under a big old fig tree, where figs fell from it and were on the ground like a blanket.

When my mother moved my youngest sibling and me back to the capital permanently, a lot of things changed. She did not continue her exceptional straw work, which included the beautiful handcrafted baskets she once made on the island.

Was I disappointed?

Yes, I was highly disappointed, because I believed if she had continued in her entrepreneurial skills, she would have advanced greatly, that she would have been surrounded by her Bahamian hand-made products, in the marketplace, or perhaps, her place; selling them to both natives and tourists, alike.

My mother, instead, as you already know, in moving to the capital, became a housekeeper, and for far longer than when she had been working for herself, as a straw vendor when she lived on the island.

Evening after evening she would come home from a long and hard day at work, and as she walked through our front door, her fatigued body was an indication that the pay she received, or did not receive was truly not worth the much effort she had put in.

According to how our mother kept our own home, I would say, surely, "The laborer is worthy of his wages" (1 Timothy 5:18, James 5:4), and at a higher rate.

Despite all that, as children, my youngest sibling and I would rush to take our mother's bag. Not to ease her from her burden; it was to search for whatever goodies might be inside it, which she never failed to bring back for us.

My mother was also a bookkeeper, and a scrap of that paper was her calculator. She would add here, and subtract there until it balanced to the amount she had to spend. Believe it or not, that total included what she had to give back to God (Genesis 28:20–22, Malachi 3:8), as well.

Having the ability to manage whatever daily or weekly salary she received, whether it was little, or less than a little, enabled our mother to pay the rent, which kept a roof over our head; put food on the table, even if she did not put any in her mouth; buy shoes for us to wear; fabric to make our clothes with; and buy any other item we needed.

Today, I know without a doubt that it was the LORD, our God, who, through her unspoken prayers, extended His hand to her (Isaiah 59:1).

My mother was a very strong-willed woman, and while my youngest sibling and I loved that about her, there were times when we truly could not appreciate her will, nor accept it. Because, at times in her steadfastness, if you did something wrong, and she felt you should be punished for it, the punishment was greater than the offense was.

To get a better understanding of what I am talking about, let me share an occasion with you: when I was a teenager, I came in late one night, and just as I stepped in the front door, I saw a stuffed pillowcase leaning to one side. As I looked down at it, I heard my mother say, "Go back to where you came from, and carry that with you!"

Shocked; I lingered in the doorway, not sure of what to do. I was afraid to step backward, and I was afraid to enter our home.

Did her anger subsided, and I was let in?

No; my mother never made amendments to her will. She meant what she said, and said what she meant.

So that night, I was put out of the house, lugging a pillowcase with my clothes in it. And at that time, it didn't dawn on me to ask my sister if she was told to pack my clothes, or if our mother herself did.

Do you know I can hear your thinking, and loudly too?

No, I was not that kind of girl. I was not out there fornicating with some guy. I would not have dared.

My mother often said to my youngest sibling and me, "If you do foolish things in here, I'll make you eat that like hog eat swill."

And let me tell you, Laura had no intentions of finding out if she meant that, as well. My back was not going to become a goat skin drum for her. I'm a fan of junkanoo, not an instrument.

I was over at one of my elder sibling's places, watching movies, and because I was enjoying myself so much; the time had totally gotten away from me. And being more afraid of my mother, than of the empty streets, late at night; when

I realized the time, I jumped up, and ran out of her front door, and headed for home, before she could have stopped me.

While walking back to my sister that night; early that morning, with my jolly bundle held tightly in front of me, I heard my youngest sibling calling out to me, in her unique way of saying my name:

"Lau, mommy said to come back!"

And who was it in the first place that told me to go?

My mother! So now leave me alone; let me "Make a page of my age." Those words were often said by our mother. I wanted my sister to give them back to her, but I kept them in my thoughts, only.

For a while, I pretended not to hear her calling me because I was still very upset with our mother. Then I thought, it is already past midnight, and the streets are bare. If something happens to either one of us, then it happens to both of us. So I turned around, and we headed back home together, chatting along the way.

While I was still upset with my mother, I knew that that was her way of showing me I could not have my way in her house, no matter where I was coming from, or what I had been doing. Her way of training, however, was for me, over the top.

Here is another occurrence, between my mother, and me:

One time, she had gotten so mad at me, and instead of just beating me, she attacked me. Before I knew what was happening, I was lying on my back on the sofa gasping for breath. Her hands were in a vice-like grip around my neck. As one of my elder siblings pulled her off me, she asked, "Mother, you trying to kill your daughter, what did Laura do?"

She could not tell my sister what I had done, or what I had even said because she did not know. Today, I am a woman with children of my own, and still, I cannot say what caused my mother to render such punishment upon me.

Nevertheless, was she that serious-minded in her discipline?

This episode that I am about to share with you occurred with my mother and one of my elder siblings. In fact, with the one who I was going back to the night when our mother put me out of her house. I have chosen to record this event in our mother's legacy because it can no longer make my sister feel embarrassed; she passed away.

Now, my youngest sibling and I were not present when it took place. So I'm recapping it, the way another one of our elder siblings told it.

One day, our sister "went out and returned home with a new boyfriend; all excited to introduce him to mother. Mother took one look at the young man, turned her head away from him, and then asked, "Where is it… because I don't see it?"

Not nice at all.

I know, but despite how humiliating that must have been for our sister, it was still ridiculously funny to us and every opportunity we got, we would find ourselves teasing her about it, and laughing uncontrollably.

An old childish saying goes like this, and you might be familiar with it; "If you don't like it, then, lump it."

Our mother used to say, "If you don't like it, then, let me see you do something about it."

Most times when our mother had a point to make, because of her willpower, she made it strong, and so, I can only imagine what would have happened to any of us, if we had tried to do something about anything, that we did not like.

My mother; oh man, I don't know. Either, she was that serious, or she just had no consideration for anyone's feelings, at all.

Now you might think this is a rhetorical question, but it is not.

Have you ever heard of anyone who got beaten even while they were praying?

Well, that was my mother, my youngest sibling, and me.

In teaching us the Lord's Prayer (Matthew 6:9–13), she showed no leniency towards us, whatsoever. For her, there was no room for errors.

My youngest sibling and I have learned through our mother, who had no patience with us, how to be patient with our children.

There were times too when we even got beaten by our mother, with her eyes. How is this possible?

Well, if you said something that she did not like, or if she saw you doing something that was displeasing to her, and she could not get to you, with an actual rod, she would tense her face, and stare at you for the longest, without blinking, or saying a word.

And we dare not ask her, "What happened, Mommy?"

You knew already what that mental look meant.

If it appeared to our mother, we were in any way, form, or fashion, giving her an attitude, you could be sure, right after she said, "I Yei boy; you get plenty of spirit stumpin', dill dosin'", something was coming at you. And whatever she threw at you, you had to pick it up and give it back to her, which was not always easy to do, because in doing so, you were going to get hit, again, and even harder.

I can at no time, in any situation, recall our mother sparing the rod with my youngest sibling, or me. And if in any case she had punished you, and found out you were truly innocent; instead of apologizing, she would say, "That's your beaten for next time. Now go and sit down, and don't let me hear your mouth in here."

When the next time, however, came, our mother had a loss of memory. We still got beaten. And since she had no conscience when beating you, you got beat with whatever she felt like beating you with, and in whichever way she chose to, and for as long as she wanted to, with the lyrics, "I'm tired of you, I'm tired of you. I'm going to kill you; you hear me, you hear me."

Ok mommy, ok mommy; I heard you, I heard you.

The cowbells were licking loudly, and rhythmically, in my ears, so how could I not hear them?

Sometimes, it was difficult for my youngest sibling, or me, to even pass freely, wherever our mother was sitting, because out of the blue, she would lift her foot to kick you, and then say, "Gone, go sit down before I don't kick you down. You look like a periwinkle in rainy weather."

Our mother was unpredictable and impulsive, and her vocabulary often mystified us.

I can recall the many times my youngest sibling and I got a tongue-lashing from her, just for looking her way.

And if either one of us were caught eyeballing our mother, after getting beaten by her, she would ask, "What happened; you looking to fight me now? Come on, try it and I'll..."

If you don't want your radical mother to finish that sentence on you, then you better quickly look the other way.

This track and field moment is one I do believe my youngest sibling and I will never forget, for as long as we both shall live. And I will allow her, however much time she needs, to forgive me for writing about it in our mother's legacy since others will now know about it:

Our mother for whatever reason, refused to take care of a matter that was starting to get to the two of us. And rather than accept that, we decided to "do something about it".

Well, isn't that what she always said, "If you don't like it, then, let me see you do something about it"?

So, we decided we were going to run away from home.

One evening when it was almost time for our mother to return home from work, we went and stood at the back door. And as soon as we heard her making her way through the front door; nervously, we looked at each other. My sister was the first to speak:

"Lau, are you coming?"

"I don't know."

"You're not coming?"

"Uh-uh!"

When our mother called out our names, my sister said:

"I'm leaving then."

She swung open the door, and in no time, she was gone.

While I was still trying to envision running away from home, she already had her mind made up. And I watched as she sprinted through the backyard as if she was competing in a sports event. And trust me, she would have won too, given her speed.

I waited until I could no longer see her, and then, I answered our mother; yes, ma'am.

"Where is your sister?"

Shocks! This woman is just too sharp. She knew it was a solo reply and not the duet she usually got when we heard both our names called to see if we were both at home.

"I don't know mommy."

"She didn't tell you where she was going?"

"No, ma'am."

"Wait until she gets her little skin back here. I told you over and over not to leave this house after you get in from school, especially when I am not here."

Our mother may not have known this, but we never did.

Maybe, you are thinking I lied to my mother, regarding my sister's whereabouts.

The truth is, while we did plan together, to run away from home, we had no idea at all, where we were going. So it was not a lie.

Dark had begun to fall, and my youngest sibling was still out there, alone

Why?

Simply because I had gotten scared and chickened out.

"Laura!" My mother called strongly, breaking into my thoughts.

I guessed she had been calling me for a while.

I rushed to her. Yes, ma'am?

"I asked you, is your sister back at home yet?"

"No, ma'am!"

Still, in a strong tone, she said to my brother, "Go out there and look for that girl; dark will soon fall."

When my brother got up to leave, I walked behind him but remained at the kitchen door, and watched as he took the same path our sister took, except he was walking, not sprinting.

While standing there, I heard, "Psst!" I peeked out the door; looked left and right, but saw no one.

When I heard it again, I then realized the sound was coming from inside So I quickly turned around, and that's when I saw my youngest sibling up in the loft. She beckoned to me, and in excitement, I hurriedly climbed up to join her After we talked for a while, I came back down and said nothing to our mother

I believe just how my sister returned to the house without any of us knowing (Mark 13:32–33), not even me (Luke 21:34–36, 1 Peter 4:7), until she made that sound (1 Thessalonians 4:16); only looking down from the loft

(Psalm 14:2–3), watching and waiting for me to enter the kitchen, Christ in like manner is going to return (1 Thessalonians 5:2).

When our brother returned home, he said, "I could not find her, Mother, and those I asked about her, did not see her, either."

Was I alarmed by any of this?

Not in the least, because I knew already, she was safely home, and so was he.

Did I use that opportunity to let our mother know where she was, even before our brother went looking for her?

No. I said nothing to her, and neither did I say anything to our brother. I just continued to study our mother, until I could see her, in my mind's eyes, without the whip she was holding, to use on my sister.

When I saw our mother's anger spin to worry, I said, 'Mommy, she is home; in the backroom.'

"Thank God!" My mother breathed out.

Those words were a breath of fresh air for her.

Let me explain. The loft was an upper level that complimented the room at the far end of our house. It was an area that only she and I had discovered, and decided we would keep quiet about it, and make it our little "pavilion" (Psalm 27:5), our little "secret place" (Psalm 31:20). And when at any time, we felt the need to get away from anything, or even anyone, together, or alone, that is where we would be.

So, to keep myself from giving away the location of our little haven, our little paradise, I purposefully said, 'She is in the back room.'

It took that distressing situation for our mother to accept that the philosophy, "Children should be seen and not heard" is by man, not God (Matthew 18:6, Mark 10:13–16).

Years later, when we suffered the loss of that very brother, due to an incident it was very hard for our mother to cope, because she was yet, again, mourning the loss of another child.

During his funeral, his son, who was just a child when his mother moved to the U.S.; taking him with her, asked, "Aunt Laura, how could you and Aunty be so calm in all this?"

He was referring to my youngest sibling.

Now although my nephew was no longer a child, he had yet to learn that one, showing calmness on the outside does not mean one is not groaning "in the spirit and…troubled". John 11:32–33

The thing is, my sister and I knew then, and we know now, Jesus is way more powerful than any storm is (Mark 4:35–41), or could be, and He had already stilled the one that had risen in us (John 16:33, 14:27), way before we got to our brother's funeral.

Yes, our brother's death was senseless, and I would say, untimely, but why should we weep and stagger "as others who have no hope" (1 Thessalonians 4:13, Romans 15:13)?

The account: we were told our brother was only trying to get another young man to understand that his actions were wrong (Romans 7:15–19), and not even in anger. But the young man, someone he knew, of course, did not care about what was right, or what was wrong (Jeremiah 2:19), only in giving birth to his wicked thoughts (2 Corinthians 13:7).

That event escalated to my mother having to watch her son on a gurney fighting desperately to hold on to his precious life.

Then, it worsened to where the doctors saw no need to give my brother any type of emergency treatment, because, among themselves, they had already declared him dead.

Confirmation of that came, when they said to her, "Sorry, ma'am, but there is nothing we can do to help your son."

After hearing those words, my mother took one long hard look at her son, lying there in a coma; touched him, turned, and then, walked away.

In her heart, she knew there was only one thing left for her to do, and that was to begin making funeral arrangements, because the doctors would soon, officially, announce him dead.

On that day, before he was taken to the hospital, I received a phone call from one of my nieces. When I answered, the words; "You better come to your brother; looks like he is dying", came sharply into my ear, and left me flabbergasted.

Call for an ambulance, I quickly said.

While driving to my brother's place, I felt much anger toward my niece, stirring up in me (Ephesians 4:26–27), but when I arrived there, and saw the state he was in, my heart became heavy with sorrow, and my niece quickly became a washed stone in the back of my mind.

Another thing that confounded me, as regards my brother's incident was an individual ran pass the Police Station, and whatever other emergency area, all the way to my mother's place, and when she got there, she cried out, "Mother, they're killing your son"!

I learned my youngest sibling was the one who responded to her, and wisely (Proverb 12:18).

That day as I walked beside my mother, down the long corridors of our local hospital; the grief that was eating away at my own heart, I knew, was only a fragment of what I saw in her walk, and even her eyes, let alone, what I could not see in her heart.

Romans 12:21 tells us "Do not be overcome by evil, but overcome evil with good." Yet, when evil meets good, many of us still allow evil to triumph over good (3 John 1:11).

As for my beloved brother, who boldly spoke out against the evil that he saw (1 Thessalonians 5:14–15), that is how he will be remembered, in our "hearts and minds through Christ Jesus" (Philippians 4:7), and not as we later learned: he had become a victim due to circumstances.

One of the many things both my youngest sibling and I knew not to do when being scolded by our mother was to not make eye contact with her. Because if you looked her in the eyes, she would ask, abrasively, "What happened; you feel like you're a woman, now?

Yet, at times, when we stood before our mother, to be disciplined, she would say, "Look at me, I'm talking to you." And if we, as much as blinked while looking at her, she would then, say, in a harsh tone, "Oh, so you're cutting your eyes at me, now."

Our mother's nit-picking at every little darn thing, was for me, very annoying. It seemed as if, when it came to us, she could always find something to nit and pick at; to get upset about, and then, beat us for it.

And yet, our elder siblings said, we got a better break from our mother than they did.

What our siblings need to know is this, our mother practiced "Spare the rod, spoil the child" on them, to become perfect at it, on us.

My mother, looking back over her life, I am certain, saw where she had taken too much destructive criticism from a lot of people, inclusive of family members, and without fighting back. (1 Timothy 1:18, 6:12)

And I could always tell when her spirit was down; when she was feeling depressed about how her life had turned out; when she was perhaps, thinking she should have made better choices for herself, and for her children, because she would say, "If I could do some things over in my life, Laura; I would, just for the sake of you all."

Those words, I believed, came straight from the very core of my mother's heart, because they melted mine. And I knew they were meant for all of her children, not just my youngest sibling, and me.

In learning as well, of the much pain others inflicted upon my mother, and how she, alone, endured it; every awful thing she was feeling, I was feeling too, and wishing I could go back in her time, to stop every bad thing that was about to happen to her, from happening; and every wrong choice that she had already made, to replace it with the right one, and not only for her sake, but also, for the sake of each one of her children.

That was not my head filled with wishful thinking; that was my heart breaking for my dear mother, who, not until late in her life, accepted the Man, who loved her with everlasting love.

When I found out that my mother had gotten married, at a very early age, and by that time, already had a child, my heart sank.

One afternoon, my youngest sibling called to let me know that she was going through some papers and came across our mother's marriage certificate.

Now despite her saying in an unusual tone, "Mommy got married at a very early age." I replied there was nothing wrong with that (1 Corinthians 7:9).

"Lau, Mommy got married at the age of fourteen!"

She uttered, distastefully.

And at that point, I realized she sounded nasal, which told me she had been crying.

What did you say? Are you serious? I asked at once.

She went on to say, "The thought of that marriage Lau."

Our mother told us so many stories about her marriage, which was troubling to hear since they were only about mistreatment (Ephesians 5:28–29). This brought me to understand why my sister "cried out to God" (2 Samuel 22:7) to get her beyond those distressing images.

So, the thought of that marriage, indeed!

With an unsettling spirit, I called our sister, who had for many years, moved away from the capital, to escape many things, and, to make a better life for herself, to ask her about our mother's age at marriage.

"Mother was not that young when she got married. Someone, somewhere along the way must have made a mistake with her age, during the registration process."

Did my sister believe that?

We were talking about the family island, where one could have at the age of fourteen, leave school, and there was nothing to it.

Therefore, our mother could have very well gotten married at such a tender age. And while I feel it is okay, for one to get married at an early age (1 Corinthians 7:1–9); I believe fourteen is still too young for marriage.

What was also disturbing about that was, my mother, by that time, already had a child. This means she became a mother, even at a younger age than when she had gotten married.

My grandparents, who lived on the island all their lives, where there is nothing but farms, gave me no reason to believe they had a liking for powdered potatoes. But after learning they had packaged their young daughter, like instant mashed potatoes, put her in a box, and then, shipped her off to some man's house, made me think differently of them. And that also explained to me why my youngest sibling and I never heard anything about how our mother was brought up; she instantly grew up!

The best choice of mashed potatoes, for me, is homemade; and if I want to have it, I cannot pour boiling water into pulverized, artificial potatoes from a box. The natural raw potatoes must be peeled, washed, cut into parts, put in a pot, with water, and then, placed on the stove, with the fire at the right level, to boil them properly, with a little garlic, or thyme added to awaken its flavor. And while I am patiently waiting for the potatoes to reach the right texture, I have my butter, cream, and a dash of salt, to mix into them, and my garnish, to give it a perfect finish.

That recipe, however, is not intended for the actual mashed potatoes. It is the method, whether tedious or not, that a father, who truly loves and cares for his daughter, will use, to ensure that she is mature and well-prepared for life, not push her out of his home, into the world, to live an adult life, prematurely.

That same marriage contract my grandfather signed off on, almost cost my mother her life, and not once, not even twice, but repeatedly. And when she ran back to the place she was put out of, for help, for safety, she was sent right back to the hellhole she was trying desperately to escape from. And I cannot help but wonder about the path she had to take, to get back to her parents' house; was it a safe and smooth one?

Or did she purposely take the path, where she had to part bushes out of her way, or maybe climb rocks, or wade through ponds, so that, if her husband had chased after her, he would not have caught sight of her?

Or better yet, find himself downright lost, somewhere along the way, and then, vanished; and she would not have to be afraid, anymore, because her husband, she "shall see again no more forever." (Exodus 14:13–14)

I am sorry, but anytime, after hearing one of my mother's distressing stories, I would find myself picturing her running in the night, with a baby in her arms, to her parents' house, believing they would shelter her, and her child. But, when she arrived there, breathless, and scared out of her wits; rather than accept her, and protect her, the way they should have, in the first place, they reminded her of the fact that she was now married, and no longer their responsibility.

And although true, being Christian parents, weren't they concerned, at all, that they married their young daughter off to some vampire, and not to a man, who was supposed to love her, the way the word of God instructs a man to love his wife (Ephesians 5:8, 1 Peter 3:7)?

I believe, if my mother had made the decision herself, to be married to this individual, and with her father already knowing the individual's spirit, no matter how much she cried, or ranted, "Papa, I love him, and I want to be his wife"; he would have hardheartedly declined, because that man would not have been right for his precious daughter.

But they were satisfied with the fact that they had signed her life over to him, and probably thought that he had the right to do whatever he wanted to her. And if that meant slapping her around to bring her to her senses, or because he had lost his senses, then, so be it.

My mother, to her parents, may have been the wayward daughter and brought shame to their Christian home, and so, by any measure, they wanted her out of the house. But, the measurements they took, I would say, placed her more, in harm's way.

My grandparents, perhaps, were ignorant of many things, and maybe, we all are, in one way, or another. But at least they should have been aware that a marriage certificate is not a license that grants permission for one spouse to abuse the other, not in words, nor action.

I can recall this episode vividly, which took place with our grandfather, whom we called Papa, and us when we were children living on the island. Through this happening, we learned that he was a no-nonsense man and that he would not tolerate anyone, "who disdains instruction". (Proverbs 15:31–33)

One night, a few of the grandchildren and great-grandchildren, including myself, had gathered around the table, in the family room, and did not realize how loudly we were talking and laughing, until our grandfather yelled from his bedroom, "Be quiet out there."

Well, we did quiet down, but I guessed, we were still too loud for him because he, again, shouted, "Be quiet out there."

Once more, we lowered our chatting, and our laughter, or we thought we did, until he bellowed a little louder, "I said, be quiet out there."

What kind of ears did our grandfather have, man?

And because we had gotten caught up, all over again, in our moments of excitement, we did not realize he had come out of his bedroom, into the room where we were. Not until we heard his walking cane slam on the table, we were sitting at.

Fright, shut us all up, immediately!

Papa looked at us for a few moments, lifted his cane from the table, and then went back into his room.

If a pin had fallen to the floor, I am sure, he would have heard it.

Grandfather's fright night; I called it.

That proved how peeved Papa was, at us. But, to think about it, what if he had, by mistake, broken someone's hand, or finger?

Proverbs 17:27 says, "He who has knowledge spares his words, and a man of understanding is of a calm spirit."

I recognized that very Scripture described my grandfather to a T.

But, while he was not a man of many words, he would, with his mesmerizing eyes, watch your every action, and then, let you know exactly what he thought of it, through his guitar, which he played every day, on the bench, under the big old fig tree.

However, I believe those hymns he played then were his way of granting his family, peace, hope, love, and a blessed assurance, for today; and I am grateful to God for it all.

You know, I am quite aware now, of where my mother got her captivating look; it was from her father.

Yet, while I loved listening to him play his guitar; the way he dealt with my mother in her young days is for me, by far, to be admired.

How is it that she came to lie with a man, or a boy, so early in her life, if her father was of an inflexible spirit?

There were too many ill-fated affairs in my mother's life; and, as for her marriage, if it was up to me; it would not have under any circumstance, any jurisdiction, law, or decree, taken place.

But, was my mother so defiant, that it drove her father to marry her off, in hopes that she would live in compliance with another man's directives (Ephesians 5:22–24, Colossians 3:18). But how, when she had yet to learn how to comply with the rules of her father (Ephesians 6:1–3, Colossians 3:20)?

Sometimes, when I think about my mother's life, I also wonder, if she in those days, had even one friend (Proverbs 18:24), whom she could have relied on. Did one person (Psalm 41:7), at least, stand by her, when she was going through? Was there no one, at all, who felt the burning desire to guide her (Proverbs 27:9), in the right direction?

Moreover, I felt like Papa and Mama, my grandparents, for being Christian parents, gave up too quickly on their daughter, who still needed to be trained and guided by them (Proverbs 22:6), and not only spiritually (Psalm 34:11) but mentally (Ephesians 6:4, Colossians 3:21), as well.

Instead, my mother, who still needed to feel her father's tender love, was driven out, to receive whatever, from another man.

My mother, who still needed to feel her mother's warm embrace, was at her young age, embracing a baby.

As I reflect on it all, I ask myself this; out of all the men she has had in her life, intimately, including her husband, and my late father, which one held her not only in his arms, but also in his heart, and loved her the way a man, truly ought to love a woman?

Her father made his mark on her life, but, as you already know, that mark for her, later, became an ugly scar.

So, tell me, how could this mother have kept herself from making so many immoral choices in her life, if she had yet to know "A Man called Jesus" (John 9:11)?

How could this mother have shown her children anything different from what she had shown them, unless, she had allowed God to take control of all that was happening in her life?

"For… all His work is done in truth. He loves righteousness and justice; the earth is full of the goodness of the LORD" (Psalm 33:4–5).

Maybe my mother did not know that, despite how cruel, how nasty, how disrespectful others could be to you, in God's "presence is fullness of joy" (Psalm 16:11), right in the face of it all. (Psalm 23:5–6)

My mother handled things in her wisdom (Proverbs 3:7–8), and not God's (James 1:5, Proverbs 18:15); and whether the decision she had made was best, right, or wrong, I am convinced, she only did what she thought was necessary to do, for her and her children to survive.

When the man whom her father signed her off to, in marriage, turned out to be a hitman, and was sentenced to death by hanging, she struggled alone, with the five children she had for him (Deuteronomy 10:17–18, Isaiah 1:17, 1 Timothy 5:5–7), which does not include the very first child she had.

You know, I loved my grandparents a whole lot, and while neither of them exist, today, another thing that I found inexplicable, regarding them, is they sent away their baby girl, through an early marriage, but became the guardians of the first child, whom she gave birth to.

And sadly, my eldest sibling had no idea, at all, who her biological mother was. Not until very late in her life.

When my mother became a widow; because of the way she lost her husband, those you did not think would call her children ill names; did.

Many looked at her life, and the only thing they saw fit to do, was criticize her and humiliate her, even more.

But, I looked into this woman's life, and saw a widow, struggling with her five young children, not only in poverty and adversity but also, in cruelty, yet still going strong.

I saw a widow, whose two sons she gave birth to, for her husband, regardless of what others may have assumed, or, how others may have judged them, or even gaveled their lives; the truth is, neither of them walked in their father's footsteps. And for this, I say, to God be the glory.

Yes; it is true! My mother, after the death of her husband, began having affairs with other women's husbands (John 4:5–30), and for this, she was called *a Samaritan woman.* But no matter how much she appeared to be *a woman of Samaria;* disappointingly for them, she was a woman of the same country as them, The Bahamas.

And although she had a child, or two; even three, from just about all of those relationships she was in, after becoming a widow; Jesus, unlike them, did not *condemn* her (John 8:3–11), nor any of the children she brought forth from those adulterous relationships.

When my youngest brother, who came forth from one of those relationships, decided, if trouble came seeking him, he was not going to hide, walk, or run away from it (Proverbs 14:15–19); I was glad to learn that when my mother scolded him for his temperament (Proverbs 9:6, 1 Peter 2:15), he packed his clothes, got on a mail boat, and headed back to the island (Proverbs 16:6–7, 16:17). And from that day to this day, that is where my brother has been living.

Again, I say, to God be the glory.

As you continue to read *my mother's legacy,* you will see that this Bahamian woman, just like *the Samaritan woman,* met a Man.

Does that mean she *left her waterpot and run?*

No; she left having a relationship with every other man, and bowed her "knees to the Father of our Lord Jesus Christ" (Ephesians 3:14)!

My mother saw how different this Man was.

She realized that He did not want to have a good time, like all the others, and then, moved on.

Her spirit told her, that if she accepted Him, as Lord and Savior of her life, He would be with her, forever. And when she did accept Him, He became the last Man in her life.

So, unlike those who judged my mother, and sentenced her before the hearing; I would have honored her, during the hearing, and even after the hearing, and not because I am her daughter. I have come to realize the only parent without faults, without failures, is God.

And when a mother says, "I wish that children came with a manual", or "A child does not come with a manual", I know already that the Holy Bible is God's manual (2 Timothy 3:16–17), and that it existed way before any child or adult, ever did (John 1:1–2)!

If a mother studies "This Book of the Law" (Joshua 1:8), persistently, she will discover that, it does not hold the power she needs, to keep the enemy away from her, and her child, or her children; in the mighty name of Jesus, it releases the power to her (Matthew 22:29).

While talking about God's manual, I was again, reminded of a time, when I was on the island, when one of my elder siblings held Bible quizzes every Sunday, with two of our eldest sibling's children, our youngest sibling, and yours truly. And we looked forward to these Sunday afternoons, because she made them so much fun.

Now, although she did not say this, I do believe her theme, although long, was straight from the Holy Bible: "Remember now your Creator in the days of your youth" (Ecclesiastes 12:1); "and that from childhood you have known the Holy Scriptures, which are able to make you wise for salvation through faith which is in Christ Jesus." (2 Timothy 3:15)

Without any of us knowing, she would purchase four items, wrap them and then, on the evening of the quiz, she would come to the table, in the family room, with her Bible, a writing pad, a pencil, and of course, those gifts.

"These prizes are for the ones who answer the most questions; correctly" she would say, and then open the Bible, and begin reading.

Now, if we wanted to win any of those prizes, we had to listen carefully and keep in mind what she had read. And my sister either had a good memory, or she simply knew the Scriptures very well, because, whenever any of us answered a question, she never looked back in the Bible, to see if we were correct, or not.

But, if we did not see her write down a point, it meant, we answered incorrectly.

When she felt she had asked enough questions, she would then calculate the points. And the gifts were always given in the order of third, second, and first place. Now, when it came to first place, she would hesitate before calling the name. So the two, whose names she did not call, would be waiting anxiously because only one could be the winner, and receive the best prize of them all.

You know, although there were four of us, there was no fourth place in her game. However, after the winner would have received his gift, the remaining gift would go to whoever answered the bonus question correctly, which means one could end up with two gifts, while another has none.

The bonus question: "Who can tell me exactly where the Scripture lesson was taken from?"

Oftentimes, no one could give the right answer, but still, we were filled with excitement for next Sunday's lesson.

Excited to learn the word of God?

No! We were excited to win the prizes.

But hey, now that I am no longer a child, I recognize the gift she gave us from the Holy Bible (Psalm 71:17–19) was far more precious than the ones she gave us, in those brown paper wrappings.

As my beloved sister is no longer with us; this was "told as a memorial to her." (Mark 14:9)

Another thing that brought us much happiness when we were children living on the island was a performance that took place once a week, in one of the schoolhouses. An elderly Christian man would come from one of the settlements, with a dummy by the name of Chocolate, and the most humorous, but instructive conversation would take place between the two of them, which had not only the children laughing, but the adults, as well; filling the entire schoolhouse with laughter.

What is even funnier; then, I believed that Chocolate was back talking to the elderly man, but he was a dummy, right!

Anyway, the old man was a blessing to our young spirit, as well.

As the years went by, my mother, of course, got older; and still looked good for her age.

There was a particular family member, who, whenever she saw my mother, would say, "Boy, your mother is one strong woman."

In my mind, I'm like, yeah, yeah; her children know that already, but please, do not stop there. Keep talking, help me to know if you were one on the island, whose door remained shut, when she ran to it and pounded on it, because she was desperately seeking shelter (Galatians 6:2–3); or when she humbly knocked on it, asking for bread, to feed her children (Deuteronomy 15:7–11).

Or maybe, she was one of *"Dem too gravalicious…"*

I learned when my mother left the island, and never looked back, not even to claim a portion of anything that belonged to her, through her parents, that when her elder children, including my brother, who now lives on the island, tried to claim our mother's inheritance; persons, even from the back of Jabiim, had already grab everything, had consumed it all, and said it was theirs (Mark 7:22–23).

And those who did not build, or knock down what was there, made it a field of fruits and vegetables; and while I thought generational properties are not to be sold, others did sell what was not even theirs to sell, but through what documents?

The reason why my mother did not look beaten up and run down, not even after she began bearing children from a very early age; not even after she suffered much abuse from her husband, physically, as well as verbally; and possibly from any other man she was involved with, after the death of her husband; not even after family members and others, closed their hearts to her, and treated her cruelly is because God did not "shut up His tender mercies" (Psalm 77:7–9) toward her.

We never failed to let our mother hear from us, especially at family gatherings how good she still looked, despite all that she had been through.

Her reply would always be "Only the good Lord is keeping your old ma."

Then we would say, "…and whom God keeps is well kept."

One of the things our mother loved to do was walk, and so, almost every where she went, she did just that. And even if she had nowhere, in particular to go, she would still go for a stroll; sometimes, twice on the same day. Then we noticed she was not walking as much as she used to.

"Mommy, are you going walking today?" We would ask.

"No, not today, love. Feeling a bit tired, probably tomorrow."

Tomorrow came, and still, she did not go walking, and this was now becoming strange. Since there were times when our mother, just to have her daily walk, would get up, and go out on the corner, to the convenience store and return with an unnecessary purchased item.

But, that was her way of treating us, and we loved it.

It seemed as if everybody in the vicinity of where we lived knew our mother, and never failed to greet her with a "Hi mother, how are you, today?"

There was a time when one of my elder siblings and I were walking with her; my sister, with much passion in her voice, said, "I mean mother knows everybody!" Our mother replied, "No, everybody knows me. Even the stray dogs; they all greet me with a bark when they see me passing by."

We had to stop walking for a few moments, to retain ourselves, because we were drunk with merriment (Proverbs 17:22).

If you had an opportunity to go walking with my mother, I am sure, you were anything, but bored.

Due to my mother's great sense of humor, when she made a joke; even if you were mad at her, it was hard to hold back your laughter.

While I found my mother to be strikingly amusing, I discovered something odd about the way she moved.

Whenever we had to move for one reason or another, we could practically carry the stuff in our hands. Because the place we were moving out from was not far from the place we were moving into.

You know, when it comes to an area, every one by right can see it however they choose to see it; in other words, judge it.

As for East Street; my mother's heart was there, and I believe this because no matter where we moved to, or how many times we moved, we were always, somehow, still connected to it. And since my youngest sibling and me, navel-strings are buried there; then, a part of us is attached to East Street, as well.

Now, although we met with hardship while living on East Street, no matter which part we lived in, we were still able to create everlasting memories, through the loving relationship we built with some of our neighbors (Galatians 5:13–15).

When our mother did move from East Street to an area that had no road at all, connecting to it, it was said by a family member, "They moved mother and made her sick."

That statement, to me, was like saying we killed our mother and was far more offensive than the nasty remarks we heard coming from some of our neighbors, regarding our old living conditions.

"No matter how old your place is; fix it up for your decency."

That was one of my mother's philosophies.

And that was why whenever anyone came over to our home, be it a family member, or a guest, it was always decent and in order.

And my mother was like this; if there was anything the landowner refused to repair, she would somehow fix it herself, despite her budget.

It seemed though, no matter which place my mother moved into, there was always something or some things that needed to be repaired.

I mean, we could never just move into a place, and right away be content. We had to do some work, here; do some work, there, which should have been done by the property owner before renting it.

Now, although my mother knew the condition of the place, but moved into it, anyway; it was because she knew the size of her pocketbook, even better.

And while I was embarrassed, then, when I learned that my schoolmates found out where I live; today, I feel much appreciation, and admiration for my dear mother, who, rather than put her basket higher than she could have reached it, said to herself, "they called me a Samaritan; I am not even a *Saul* (Acts 13:9), but a *Paul,* "I have learned in whatever state I am, to be content" Philippians 4:11–13

But, doesn't it grieve your spirit to know that, there are landowners, who no matter how badly their building might need repairs, that are even noticeable or, no matter what kind of living conditions their tenants might be enduring even after being told; as long as they can collect the rent from them, whether monthly, weekly, daily, or even hourly, they are the only ones, at the end of the day, pleased.

Speaking of paying rent; oh man, let me tell you, my mother was a perfectionist in paying hers; even if it meant having to scrape the rice or the flour canister. And no matter how hard she scraped either one, you never heard the scraping sound, but you knew that she scraped it, when you were served your portion of the meal.

"Always pay your rent, even if you have to go to bed hungry.

That was another one of my mother's philosophies.

In other words, it is better to be hungry than to be humiliated.

As the days went by, my mother's spirit for walking also went by.

She no longer had interest in it.

Now, although she humored us when we joked about it, and we would all laugh, no one had the slightest idea of what was happening to her. So again, as you continue to read *my mother's legacy*, you will see that it was not us, but God, who moved her from where she was, into a place that was more accommodating for what befell her.

Our mother losing her drive for walking was no longer our only concern. We now realized whatever she ate came back up, minutes later.

And when that started happening, she found herself going for checkups, more than usual; receiving prescription after prescription for what the doctors diagnosed as gastritis and low blood pressure.

My mother filled every prescription, followed every instruction, and kept every appointment she was given. Yet, her state remained the same.

By this time, she had become "A walking pharmacy", and was still, always under the weather.

Whatever was suppressing my mother's health would at times cause her body to go into an irrepressible state, which I saw for the first time when she and I were on an outing in Rawson Square.

"I'm not feeling well", she said.

We can leave, I replied.

"No. I'll just sit down for a while."

Although we had gotten to the event before it started, we still could not find any vacant chairs, and so, we had been standing for quite some time. I walked away, slowly with her; looking around, hoping to find an empty chair somewhere. A gentleman who noticed me, asked, "You need a seat for her; she can sit here." As he got up, I said thank you.

I stayed at my mother's side, and from there, I tried to see the event, but the view was not as good as where we had been standing.

My mother, recognizing I could not see the performance, said, "You go back to where we were; I'll stay here for a while."

Are you sure? I asked her.

"Yeah. Go ahead, I'll be ok."

Shortly after I returned to our initial spot, I felt someone patted me on the shoulder. When I turned around, a lady said, "The woman who came with you, I think something happened to her."

I quickly thanked her; and as I headed back towards my mother, the only thing that had speed on me was not "The Bahamas Golden Girls" at the Sydney Olympics. It was "the lightning that flashes" (Luke 17:24). As I got closer, I could see her lying on the ground, and her body convulsing.

Not sure of what was happening to her; in fright, I hurriedly lowered myself to the ground, took hold of her head, and rested it on my lap. And suddenly, I became ill at ease, because there were so many onlookers. For them, my mother had become the event in Rawson Square that day.

Rather than go looking for a seat for her to sit down on, why didn't I just walk her straight to the car, and drive home where she could have lie down?

Was the question that for a long time, gnawed away at my insides.

The most unusual thing about my mother's condition was that, no matter which doctor saw her, or how many doctors saw her, their diagnoses were all the same.

"Our results show that everything is fine with your mother, but your mother's blood count is very low. Make sure she continues to take her medication and follow the diet plan we gave her."

And she did both, consistently.

But just as the doctors' analysis never changed, my mother's condition never changed, either. Perhaps, whatever was written on my mother's medical chart by the last doctor who had seen her, not examined her, is what the doctor who came after, went by.

Truly, how long does it take for one's blood count to be normal, again, or for an upset digestive system to settle down, especially, if being treated?

No physician, I believed, took the time to thoroughly examine my mother, nor could uncover what the naked eyes could not have seen.

All who saw her, again, not examined her, gambled with her life, and lost, leaving her at stake.

For quite some time, my mother had been talking about taking a trip, and it was agreed upon by all that now would be a good time for her to do so. But despite how beautiful and relaxing, or how transfixing the sights are on the island where she was born, that was not where she wanted to go.

So a few days later, she was on a flight, with one of my nieces, heading to the U.S., to enjoy a mini vacation.

Unfortunately, it turned out to be a whole lot more than that for my mother.

Whatever illness was trying to take over her life, raised its ugly head again and she had to be taken to the hospital. Where this time, a thorough examination was carried out, and what was discovered stunned even the doctors who had examined her. When my niece, whom my mother had traveled with, called, her words sent shockwaves through the family:

"Mother is in the hospital, she was diagnosed with cancer. There is a tumor in her stomach the size of a grapefruit, and it has consumed a great percentage of her blood. Once they get her blood back to a satisfactory level, they will perform surgery to remove it."

The next thing I knew, I was walking on America's soil, not knowing what to expect, or what I was going to say to my mother when I saw her.

But, after meeting, and talking with her doctors, no one had to tell Laura who it was that kept her mother standing, walking, and going strong, while traveling into that country.

No one had to tell Laura how real, or how good God is, because Laura knows this for herself (Isaiah 40:28–31).

"The quantity of blood we found in your mother's body is not sufficient for anyone to survive on. We don't see how she made it this far on her own without fainting or having a seizure."

The Oncologists could not see how, but I saw how and will tell anybody; no, I will tell the whole wide world that my mother had to survive. Because the drop of blood they found in her body was not her own, it was the blood of Jesus.

You know, I cannot say what was more shocking for her children.-

What she was ill with, or the fact that out of all the many checkups she went for to our local hospital, and, was even taken to be examined by a private doctor, and not one of them with their ranking title had the gift to perceive that our mother's condition was life-threatening, and was rapidly, getting worse.

Their arrogance made us ignorant, and somewhat imprudent, to how ill she was.

When my mother's attending physician asked, "Has she ever been seen by a doctor in The Bahamas?"

More times than I can count, I replied.

"I do not understand", he said.

Neither do I, doctor, neither do I.

The doctors called my mother "A walking miracle."

I called her my greatest inspiration, because, while a tumor was living off her blood, she was still going resiliently on the blood of Christ Jesus.

On the day of my mother's surgery, my nephew, who lives in the U.S., met up with my niece and me. And despite it being on a grave occasion, I was still glad to see him.

After we had been waiting for a while, a nurse came out, to escort us to where she was, to allow us to say what we needed to before she was taken into the operating room.

As we stood around my mother, expressing our love, and encouraging words to her, I tried my best to not let her see how heavy my heart was, because although she looked pretty calm laying there, her heart could have been heavier than mine. Only God knows what prayer was in her heart; it could have been a prayer for herself, or her children, or maybe for both her and her children.

Yet, I thought, if God brought her this far, then He was going to take her the rest of the way.

Before we left my mother's side to go back into the waiting room, we were advised by her doctors to not build our hopes up too high. The surgery was not to free her from cancer, as it had already spread; it was only to remove the tumor that was repeatedly consuming her blood.

But you know what, it was too late for the doctors to tell me, not to build my hopes up too high, because my hope was already in God, and I was not taking it back down. But I appreciated how during the surgery, we did not have to sit and wait for long hours, wondering how the procedure was going. There was a system in place that enabled us, from time to time, to check on the status

When one of my elder siblings, and one of my nieces, who is not her daughter at different times, showed up, I cannot recall at what point, and although both their stays were pretty short, their presence still meant a lot to me.

After the surgery, was I expecting my mother to, in a few hours, wake up and be back to her normal self?

Yes, but she was in a coma for a very long time, and because her condition had sunk so low, her attending physician met with my niece and me, not to discuss how we were going to pay her skyrocketing bill. They wanted us to sign papers so that if things did not look up for her by a certain time, my signature and my niece's signature as a witness, would have permitted them to pull the plug

Now, while the doctors could not pull the plug without our signatures. God could, without our prayers, pull back her "spirit" (Ecclesiastes 12:7).

For "in whose hand is the life of every living thing, and the breath of all mankind?" Job 12:10

In knowing where the answer lies, my niece and I, and family members that were back at home, began praying more earnestly for my mother; because life and breath are in God's hand (Deuteronomy 32:39), the One who "answered our prayer." Ezra 8:23

When my niece and I, again, met with the doctors, it was to agree to have them move my mother from the hospital to a place where we were told, "She would have round-the-clock service, to make whatever time she has left, as comfortable as possible." And so, following much paper transaction, she was medically transported to a Hospice by the Sea.

When my niece and I arrived there, many activities were going on. After getting through what seemed like endless red tape, we were escorted into a tranquil area, and into the room where they had already settled my mother. I could not have appreciated their prompt and efficient service more than I did.

Now, as peaceful, and as beautiful as it was there, and like they said you would, I did get an at-home feeling, but I did not feel like that was where God wanted my mother to spend her last days. I strongly felt He was not going to allow her body to be carried home in a box.

One evening when my niece and I visited my mother, I entered her room, alone. By this time, she was no longer in a coma; she was just lying there, sleeping naturally, and peacefully. Instead of disturbing her, I quietly sat down, looked upon her, and then, took a picture of her, and she was still as beautiful as ever. But, there was a big difference between the woman in the photo and the one I kept seeing in my dream.

In my dream, my mother was still vibrant, humorous, and walking to wherever she wanted to go; she was still a hard worker, and that strong disciplinarian, whom my youngest sibling and I feared, in more ways than one, yet, loved, dearly. In my dream, I saw my mother enjoying her mini vacation to the fullest, just as she said she would. She was talking and laughing, not on her native soil but on America's soil.

But the photo portrayed a woman, whom the doctors warned, memory would come and go; it represented a woman, who, even in her consciousness could not recognize her daughter, who was right at her bedside, let alone, the rest of her children who were back home; it told of a woman, who remembered everyone, and every event, but now, could not remember her birthday; it showed a woman, who, yesterday, packed her suitcase, and moved by her freewill, but now, has to be dressed, and moved by another.

Whenever my mother's mind was stable, it was the perfect opportunity for my niece and me to hold a normal conversation with her. But what she talked about mostly was how well, "All, all, black and white" that came to her aid, treated her. And this, we saw for ourselves, in both the hospital and Hospice by the Sea.

As I sat there, looking intently at my sleeping mother, I knew right then and there that her life and the lives of her children would never be the same.

The thought of that started a war in my head; the clinking sounds of the *what ifs* and the *buts* going at it, would have driven me mad, too, had it not been for the Lord (Psalms 28:6–7, 62:6–7).

Whatever time the doctors thought my mother had left to live, I guessed went way beyond that, and so, they discharged her, with the advice that she was not in any condition to travel back home, just yet, that she was still under their orders.

Beneficially for us, my niece, at the time, was living in the U.S., and for this, I give God the highest praise. Hallelujah!

Now even though a nurse came from time to time to check up on my mother, it was her children's turn to watch over her, and to care for her 24/7. And while caring for her, I watched how she in a short time became completely frail and bedridden. I observed how her condition, many times, got the better of her. I saw how she began to hallucinate, which made her chat for long periods about all sorts of things; things that half the time I had no idea of whom, or what she was talking about, let alone my niece. But we responded to her as if we knew.

There was one occasion when we were responding to her, and it seemed as if she was in sync with us, but something she said after, made us realize she was again, hallucinating. My niece and I both continued to acknowledge her, nonetheless; and surprisingly, the whole thing had become quite amusing for the two of us.

One morning, after having bathed and fed my mother, I went into the living room and sat down for breakfast. I was just about finished when I heard the Spirit say, "Go into the bedroom and check on your mother."

When I reached the doorway, I heard gasping sounds coming from her. Nervously, I rushed into the room, at her bedside, to see what was wrong. Her mouth was twisted to one side, and one of her hands was in a deformed position.

"God, please help me!" I said in desperation.

I knew very well that they were signs of a stroke.

"No krump moves allowed in here; devil, get out of my way!"

I dashed to the telephone and quickly dialed 911.

"What is your emergency?"

I could hear myself describing my mother's state, and I had to remain on the line until an ambulance arrived.

While I was impressed with the time in which it happened, I was not at all pleased with the way the two EMTs carried out my mother; neither of them showed any kind of courtesy (1 Peter 3:8), at all.

What was in their hearts (Psalm 44:21, Proverbs 14:10), and minds (Psalm 94:11), as they assisted my mother, I do not know. But I knew both my heart and my mind were saying, 'where there is life, there is hope' (Lamentations 3:21–24). And because I was very grateful they were there, to attend to her (Galatians 5:13–14), I said nothing about how I felt, not to them, and neither to anyone when we got to the hospital.

Besides, I could not let that one thing prevail over all the good that had already been shown to my mother, since she had been receiving medical attention in a country that was not her homeland. And truly, the kind assistance she received while in both the hospital and Hospice by the Sea was unlike any I had ever seen before.

One of the nurses who aided my mother in the hospital, said, "Your mom is very pretty and easy to attend to, I like her."

Also, the nurse who came to do the checkups, when she was discharged from Hospice by the Sea, asked, "Are you all from The Bahamas? When I said yes, she then made mention of how much she loves our Junkanoo culture, and that she knows people who applied for resident status in my country.

So, was I going to let those two EMTs who lacked compassion while carrying out their duties, become a thorn in my spirit? No!

After the doctor had spoken to me, about my mother; he, and the nurse that was with him, commended me for not panicking, and for immediately calling 911.

When my mother received help, right away, which prevented her from suffering irreversible damage from a stroke, it was not because I did not panic or that I instantly called 911; neither is correct.

The truth is, when the Spirit of God sent me into her room, God was already rapidly at work. And when I cried out desperately to God, He answered me long before someone through the emergency contact did.

So, all the glory belongs to God, not man, or thing (Isaiah 42:8).

Also, I am sure many back at home were still praying for my mother's healing, as well. While some believed, that she was going to return home in a box, but were made to know "God is not the God of the dead, but of the living. (Matthew 22:32)

That's why, when my niece and I were on a cruise ship with my mother, who was in a wheelchair due to her condition and could not fly, heading back to our native land, The Bahamas, I knew without any doubt that God had performed another miracle in her life, and for His "own sake" (Isaiah 48:11), He did it.

The ship, unlike the plane, was equipped with a cabin, giving my mother a welcomed opportunity to lie down and sleep, and not remain in the wheel chair. My niece and I lie awake for a very long time, talking about this and that before falling asleep.

Although our journey was for only one night, it felt much longer than that, but, can my little miserable feelings be compared to the long traumatic experience my mother had gone through?

While on the cruise ship, I also thought about my youngest sibling, whom my mother lived with before she traveled. How was she bracing herself for this huge task that was now coming to her? A task I knew well, what all it entails. Is she prepared for it; and not only physically, but also mentally?

If I say to you that my youngest sibling and I never contemplated putting our mother into a home—that would indeed, be a lie.

What happened is, every avenue we tried, failed, and I believe "This was the LORD'S doing" (Psalm 118:23, Ephesians 6:2–3), as well.

When we finally arrived at my sister's place, and our mother was all settled in her room, I looked upon her with a broken heart and then walked away to talk to my sister. As I explained to her the things that she needed to know, my heart toward her was also heavy, and this told me, that being back at home, with the rest of the family did not mean my job in helping our mother had ended.

And so, I continued to assist alongside my youngest sibling and her son, and one of our elder siblings, who, although married, on numerous occasions, made our youngest sibling's home, her home.

One of my regrets is while my mother was in my care, she had a fall, and it left a contusion on her face.

How unfortunate.

Yes. And the thought of that troubles my spirit, even today, because it only tells me I was careless, and I could not stop asking God to please forgive me.

Was she putting up a fight, and then slipped?

No, I let go of her, without making sure, she was sitting properly in the lavatory. So we moved to what was a better option.

Another thing that we kept failing at was trying to get a community nurse to come and visit our mother, so that she could, at times, receive professional help.

It was not until after many attempts, and a long tedious, pointless process, we then succeeded, but much sooner than we had expected, the visits were aborted.

Many times, I heard my mother say, "I don't ever want to get ill to the point where my children have to do everything for me."

This may sound somewhat out of the ordinary, but I believe it is not always what we want, but sometimes, what we need, and that is why God allows it to happen (Romans 8:28). Because, while many might see a situation like this, as unendurable, and shun assisting, God sees it as something that can put a broken family back together again, and bring healing to the heart of each one.

Yes, caring for our mother was rather strenuous, but neither of us, who served her, allowed our personal feelings to get in the way.

As for her, we knew she was in a lot of pain, but not once did she say that she was. She never chided about her condition, not to us, nor to anyone who visited her. Our mother proved the good LORD indeed was keeping her; that her *eyes were lifted to the hills* (Psalm 121:1–2).

The first time our mother said, "I thank you all for taking care of me; God is going to bless you all," we were so touched that our eyes became filled with tears. *Mommy* was all we could have uttered.

Whenever our mother's mind was stable, she would express her gratitude to us. And even when she had no memory of who we were, she would still give thanks to those who were serving her, especially to Jesus, the One, who served her best (Mark 10:45).

"Safe In The Arms Of Jesus" and "LORD, I'm Coming Home" were two of our mother's favorite songs.

Our mother never failed to say, "You all don't worry about me; I'll "be absent from the body and…present with the Lord" (2 Corinthians 5:8, Psalm 116:15, Ecclesiastes 12:7).

I realized whenever she heard the words from Isaiah 41:10, being read to her, her face would light up.

I later found the words of that very Scripture written on a piece of paper, in her handwriting, and I am sure she wrote it before she took ill.

Rather than discard it, it is for me, today, a memorabilia; and it is read each morning, in my daily worship.

"Sometimes, she is going to be in a lot of pain. I will give you something to give her for that", was one of the things the doctor said to us before we left the U.S.

Well, the doctor did not give us something; he gave us some things, because we brought back home a satchel of medications.

Did my mother at any time try to fight against what was happening to her, or show some kind of fear?

No, and no; my mother knew the healer had called for her (Isaiah 54:4–8), and so, through "the peace of God, which surpasses all understanding" (Philippians 4:7), she silently and courageously answered Him (2 Corinthians 4:16–18).

I know this because she no longer wanted to take the medication man had prescribed for her, yet was able to endure whatever pain was afflicting her body.

And the same peace that my mother received from God, I allowed it to flow right into my own heart and mind.

That is why when she was again admitted into the hospital, I had no fear at all of what the doctors might, or might not discover, because God Himself had already "done all things well." (Mark 7:37)

So, were we expecting any more miracles on our mother's behalf?

No, we were not!

What we were expecting, though, was for the doctors, whom we had already met with, to finally be conversant with the facts. But once again, they shocked us with their defibrillator.

"Your mother has cancer, and we cannot operate on her, because it has already spread through her body; there is nothing we can do for her."

And the doctor, who stood alongside the one, who spoke, was nodding her head in agreement. Sadly, none was the wiser.

Synchronizing; my youngest sibling's head turned to face me, and mine turned to face her, and the expression on her face said, seriously!

And I know without a doubt, mine said the same.

The news they gave us was definitely from an old newspaper.

Now, whether it was the Tribune (242) or Guardian (242), I do not know.

What I do know is this; if they had checked our mother's medical records, which were received from us when she was admitted, they would have known that this woman already had major surgery.

That once again, told me, no doctor had even taken the time to examine our mother, because if they had, the surgical scar would have been discovered, and they would have spared themselves from such humiliation.

Recalling again, the many blessings God had already bestowed upon our mother, and also upon us, now was not going to make me forget any of them, by being discourteous. So, I threw a meaningful look at the two juvenile-looking doctors that stood in front of us, both in white jackets way larger than themselves, and said, politely, when she came to you, a binder with her medical records also did. It is obvious that no one took the time to go through it before coming to speak with us.

My sister and I watched, as they now went into synchronize mode.

The evening my mother passed away, was the very evening I had no mind for going to the hospital to see her, and so, I purposely lingered on at work.

Maybe fear in one way, or another, got hold of me.

One of the HR Managers, recognizing I was still there, asked, "Are you going to visit your mother this evening?"

In a depressing tone, I said to her, I do not feel like it. And my youngest sibling called a while ago to say that the hospital wants the family there, as soon as possible.

"To be at your mother's bedside when she dies is a blessing. You don't have to believe me, but I am telling you what I know. You were the one with her in the U.S., right?"

Yes! I said.

"Well, you cannot stop now, go to the hospital and see your mother. God will bless you for it, trust me."

Her words I could not easily embrace, yet I will not forget them.

We were talking about the woman whom I have called mommy, all my life, and love dearly. And although terminally ill, how could seeing her die, be a blessing to me? How?

But, who does not want to be blessed by God?

As I was about to leave work for the hospital, which was only a few blocks away, the phone rang. When I answered, my youngest sibling said, "Wait for us; we're coming to get you."

What impeccable timing.

Excitedly, I said thank you and hung up.

As I made my way out of the office building, into the cool October breeze with the warm sunshine upon my face, I could see, despite it all, it was indeed a good evening, a beautiful day. And the feeling I got from being alive was too wonderful to deny or not describe: God's sweet love flowed down gently through the air and rested right upon me like soft velvet petals, like sweet droplets of summer rain.

Just as my family pulled into the middle parking lot, I reached the stairway.

Again, what perfect timing!

As I walked briskly toward them, I knew I wouldn't be able to hide the love and joy I felt when I saw them, not even for a million dollars.

Why?

Well, despite the love I saw coming right back at me, through the wide smiles I saw on their faces, I would have convinced myself that I was going to be paid with counterfeit.

Again, why?

In Luke 8:16–17, it says, "No one, when he has lit a lamp, covers it…"

Also, they made me realize "There is no fear in love; but perfect love casts out fear, because fear involves torment. But he who fears has not been made perfect in love" (1 John 4:18). Yet, "I am fearfully and wonderfully made… and that my soul knows very well." (Psalm 139:14)

While on our way to the hospital, I knew no matter what awaited us there God's Spirit (Zechariah 4:6) was already at hand because I felt Him amongst us (Matthew 18:19–20).

When we arrived at the hospital, and at our mother's bedside, she was lying in a fetal position, facing the entranceway, but her eyes were closed.

From the look on her face, she was either in a lot of pain or a lot was on her mind. I looked at her for a few moments, through the broken pieces of my heart, and then picked up the Holy Bible, and began reading prayerfully to her from the Book of Psalms.

Afterward, I started singing another one of her favorite songs; "Pass Me Not, O Gentle Savior"; not caring how I sounded, or how others looked on. When I saw my mother's face begin to relax, I knew at that moment she was in her sound mind, so I bent over, put one arm around her, and softly said, Mommy, I love you, but please, let go; do not hang on any longer. God said it is now time for you to leave this world.

Weakly, she signaled her hand, and although I did not know what she meant; on purpose, I said to my brother, who drove us to the hospital, Mommy wants to say something to you, and I hurriedly moved out of the way, to allow room for him to get closer to her.

I thought if our mother was hearing me, then, she also heard the voice of her firstborn son, who was likewise, present at her bedside.

After our eldest sibling (the one who had lived with our grandmother) passed away, he then became the eldest.

Now, although our mother's gesture could have meant something else, that was the reason why I stepped back, and pushed him into the forefront.

He bent toward her and asked, "What is it, mother?"

She murmured something to him that I could not understand. Moments later, her whole body started shaking. Nervously, we called out across the floor to the nurses' station, and instantly, a nurse was at her bedside. She placed one hand gently upon our mother until her body had settled. When it did, she looked at her watch, then, up at us, dipped her head, and quickly drew the curtains, to close off our mother's area.

When my brother walked away, I stood there, still looking at her. When I turned to leave, the nurse asked, "Do you want to stay awhile longer?"

"No, that's okay," I replied.

As I walked out from behind the curtains of my mother's bedside, my voice made an intense sound in the room, and my knees gave way, almost hitting the floor. A nurse suddenly appeared—I do not know from where—and rushed to my side, though she was carrying *fruit in her womb*. She took hold of my arm, and guided me to a chair, in a small office room. While passing me some Kleenex, she asked, "Was that your mother?"

Yes, I answered.

"I'm sorry for your loss. Wait here until a doctor comes to speak with you all." After I thanked her, she left.

My mother was born in October, and passed away in the same month, just several days before her seventy-fifth birthday.

The Scriptures say, "The days of our lives are seventy years; and if by reason of strength they are eighty years, yet their boast is only labor and sorrow; for it is soon cut off, and we fly away" (Psalm 90:10).

Therefore, I will inhabit hope, not discouragement.

God in His infinite "mercy… and compassion (Romans 9:14–17) saw that our mother had no strength to go the extra miles; the extra days that is, though few, that she truly had endured enough, and therefore, freed not only her, but also her children from a tiresome journey (Ecclesiastes 7:1–3).

"For if we believe that Jesus died and rose again, even so God will bring with Him those who sleep in Jesus… Therefore comfort one another with these words". 1 Thessalonians 4:13–18

Yet, at our mother's funeral, we heard words like:

"Your mother is in a better place now."

"Your mother has gone to be with the Lord, now."

"Your mother is looking down upon you all."

I know those words were said in sincerity, but according to the Holy Bible, I also know, they could not be further from the truth.

"For the living know that they will die; but the dead know nothing… for the memory of them is forgotten… nevermore will they have a share in anything done under the sun" (Ecclesiastes 9:5–6, Daniel 12:2–3). For "in that very day his plans perish" (Psalm 146:4, Revelation 14:13), and "the dust will return to the earth as it was, and the spirit will return to God who gave it" (Ecclesiastes 12:7, John 5:24–29, 1 Corinthians 15:35–57).

My mother lived for about a year after she was diagnosed with cancer, and whether she was up, or down; every day she survived it, she remembered to give thanks and praise to God, through Jesus Christ her Lord. And how could she not remember to give thanks to Him?

When close friends, and even family members for whatever reason could not find the time to visit her, not even while she was on her sickbed; or to attend her funeral, God never left her, for no reason (Romans 8:35–39). He was with her in "the Beginning and the End" (Revelation 21:6), because that's who God is…

That night, while we were heading home from the hospital, every few minutes, my brother would say, "Mother gone, mother gone," and each time I heard him say it, I was tempted to ask him, "Who's your mother?"

But I could not bring myself to ask him such a hurtful question, because my heart knew no matter how the relationship may have been between this woman, and each one of her children, she was still mother, or mommy, to them all. And if any of them has a need, or even a want, to call on her, now, no matter how deafeningly, she cannot answer.

Still, in the midst of it all, her children should have peace, since their mother on more than one occasion, said, "I see a man dressed in all white, motioning to me to come to Him." Because, in many cases, when people are dying, they tend to see nothing but evil spirits, darkness, and die without knowing Jesus Christ, as their Lord and Savior.

When I arrived home to my apartment, many thoughts were dancing in my head: maybe God allowed my mother to return home with breath in her body, to give her a chance to make peace with her children, whom she had to.

Possibly, the medicines; forgiveness, and reconciliation, He gave her to drink He offered her the opportunity, to give them to her children, to drink, as well.

Because, although she had her shortcomings as a mother, He knew that the children also had theirs.

So, when she called for each one of her children, at her bedside, to seek from them forgiveness, and to reconcile, whoever did not go to her, to be administered to, or did go, but rejected the medication, because they felt it had long expired, then, that's on them (Matthew 18:15–18, Mark 11:25–26), and not her!

I was hoping to share with you the words my mother whispered to my eldest brother on the day of her passing, but I could not since he was not able to interpret what was said.

Before I close *my mother's legacy,* I would like to share one last thing with you. When it comes to religious leaders (Ephesians 4:11–12, 1 Timothy 3:1–13, 1 Corinthians 14:34–35), I believe we all have our preferences, my mother most certainly had hers.

Now, even though she was a member of a church that blessed her heart tremendously with many great sermons, which she would joyfully talked about when she got back home. My mother also enjoyed the preaching of a minister from another church, and despite trying very hard to keep this a secret, she couldn't. Here is how she, herself, revealed it:

About 6:00 a.m., on a Thursday morning, before daylight, my youngest sibling and I heard this anxious and excited voice whispering "You all, get up, get up; I need you to hear this man preach!"

Straightaway, we were up, and filled with excitement, as well.

Let me tell you, that minister made such an impact on us; our mother did not have to concern herself with waking us up the following Thursday morning. When she called our names; before she could finish her sentence, in unison, we answered, 'listening,' and we all laughed.

And we did not have to ask for the volume to be turned up. As usual, she had it pumped right up because she wanted her neighbors to hear it as well.

During a family meeting, in preparation for our mother's funeral, we were surprised to learn that one of our cousins is a minister in that very church. And when we told him about how much our mother loved his leader's fiery sermons, the same as we do, he extended an invite.

And there was no need for him to wonder if we were going to show up, since we like listening to, and watching the actions of any minister, who was made "a flame of fire" (Psalm 104:3–4), by God.

As we sat in church that beautiful Sunday morning, anticipating the sermon and seeing the man of God behind it, our cousin took us completely by surprise with the welcome. In a very charismatic way, he let all the other worshippers know who his two cousins were, and exactly why they were there. As for the Praise and Worship Team, they were the fans that kept our hearts ablaze for what was to come, by way of the sermon.

Since the passing of our mother, my youngest sibling and I have become even more appreciative of ministers of the gospel, who are not afraid of speaking the Word, as it is written, and "are not carnal but mighty in God for pulling down strongholds, casting down arguments and every high thing that exalts itself against the knowledge of God". (2 Corinthians 10:1–6)

As I bring *my mother's legacy to a close,* I say this; for those who said, out of all the children, our mother loved my youngest sibling and me more; the truth is, we are the ones who simply stayed by her side more.

And although she is gone; the joyous moments we shared with her, at home and on our outings; our times of agreements, and disagreements that helped us to know one another better; her memorable laugh, and her unforgettable smile that made her eyes twinkle; her beauty, and refinement; the clothes she sewed; the meals she cooked, and baked for us, will always remain in our treasure boxes; our hearts.

"So I said,

"Oh, that I had wings like a dove!
I would fly away and be at rest."

Psalm 55:6

"The days of our lives are seventy years;

And if by reason of strength they are
eighty years, Yet their boast is only labor
and sorrow; For it is soon cut off, and
we fly away."

Psalm 90:10

Chapter 2

Words of Life

"Before I formed you in the womb I knew you;
Before you were born I sanctified you; I ordained you"
(Jeremiah 1:5), to lift up my name, to bring Me glory,
Not self, nor another, nor the world.

"And it happened, as He spoke these things, that a
Certain woman from the crowd raised her voice and
Said to Him, "Blessed is the womb that bore You,
And the breasts which nursed You!"

But He said, "More than that, blessed are
Those who hear the word of God and keep it!"
(Luke 11:27–28, Mark 16:15–17, John 3:14–21)

Seeds from God

"I f you, as a mother, were given the job "to seek and search out

By wisdom" (Ecclesiastes 1:13), information about a type of seed,

And to then sow it, where would you go to gather your facts?

Would you look in a dictionary?"

"Maybe not; dictionaries are filled with shortcuts.

They are just an accumulation of easy sayings."

"Then, what about an encyclopedia? It has more details."

"Haven't you heard that technology has superseded encyclopedias?

They now only look good in our library, or on our bookshelves.

So absolutely not!

"And since you feel the same way about the Holy Bible;

That the Scriptures are also a thing of the past,

You would also technologize!"

"Of course, I would; it's a common thing to do, today. Everyone does it."

"And when you, by way of the internet, find these seeds: the Word
(John 1:1, Matthew 24:14), the earth's (Genesis 1:11–12, 1:29, 2:5–6),
And man's (Genesis 4:1–2, 4:17–18, 38:6–10), which either, you
Can easily compile your information from, where would you say
It *all* came from?"

"I would say it came from man. Man placed it all there for our use."

"And I could not agree with you, more.
Man did put it there after he gathered it all from the Holy Scriptures,
But, the originator of every type of seed there is, except the
Seed of "discord" (Proverbs 6:12–19, Hebrews 12:14–15), is God.

The seed of discord is from the enemy and should not be sown
By anyone, because wherever it exists "confusion and every evil
Thing are there" (James 3:13–16). Remember, our "God is not the
Author of confusion but of peace" (1 Corinthians 14:33),
"of power and of love and of a sound mind." (2 Timothy 1:7)

Bear in mind as well, God did not just give these seeds to us,
He also provided us with all the facts that we need to know about them.
And one amazing fact is this: "the Root" (Revelation 22:16) had
existed long before any of us even planted a seed; be it in the ground
(Isaiah 30:23, Nehemiah 10:35), the womb (Genesis 17:16, 25:24,
Psalm 128:1–4), or the heart (Matthew 13:1–43, Hebrews 4:12).

Another amazing fact; while a plant needs water, air, sunlight,

And nutrients from the soil to grow to maturity; we need only one

Thing, to do the same, and that is to fully comply with the Word of

God (Deuteronomy 30:8–10, Joshua 1:8). For "In the way

Of righteousness is life, and in its pathway there is no death"

(Proverbs 12:28).

So, as you do your research, mother, using the internet,

Whether it be through your cellular phone, computer, or any

Other gadget, rather than the Holy Bible, the Good Book, itself,

You should know that you will find more than spiritual and

Wholesome seeds. You will also come across many different

Types of corrupted seeds planted there by the enemy (Luke 6:43–45).

Therefore, I say to you, be very careful of the seed you choose,

For planting, "for whatever a man sows, that he will also reap.

For he who sows to his flesh will of the flesh reap corruption,

But he who sows to the Spirit will of the Spirit reap

Everlasting life." (Galatians 6:7–8)

For us to sow to the Spirit, and not our flesh; for us to reap

Everlasting life, and not corruption, let us through God's Laws,

God's commands, learn the difference between the three seeds

He has given to mankind:

1. When planting a seed so that we may have bread to eat (Isaiah 55:10–11), we are free to plant them anywhere we want. In fact, not only one person, but as many as we want, can help us scatter them all over the earth.

2. When planting a seed that could bring forth another human being, God, our heavenly Father, expects the emitting to be done by one sower (Deuteronomy 23:2), only.

3. The most important of all; when planting a seed to grow a relationship with God (John 3:1–21, 5:38–40, Acts 2:38–39), we must each day, by faith (Matthew 17:20, Mark 4:30–32), *abide in* the Son of God (John 15:1–10), for He is *the Root* that can cultivate our hearts (Psalm 51:10, Ezekiel 36:26–28), to be "a fountain of water springing up into everlasting life." (John 4:13–14)

"Now may He who supplies seed to the sower, and bread for food,

Supply and multiply the seed you have sown and increase the

Fruits of your righteousness, while you are enriched in everything

For all liberality, which causes thanksgiving through us to

God." (2 Corinthians 9:10–11).

"A Wellspring of Life"

*I*sn't it amazing how when it comes to the Holy Bible, one Scripture can define our entire life, let alone many?

Psalm 127 for example; speaks of our house, our labor, our city, our sleep, our getting up, our heritage, and of our youth.

Let me ask you, which of the following verses, question your livelihood?

¹ "Unless the LORD builds the house, they labor in vain who build it; unless the LORD guards the city, the watchman stays awake in vain.

² It is vain for you to rise up early, to sit up late, to eat the bread of sorrows; for so He gives His beloved sleep.

³ Behold, children are a heritage from the LORD, the fruit of the womb is a reward.

⁴ Like arrows in the hand of a warrior, so are the children of one's youth.

⁵ Happy is the man who has his quiver full of them; they shall not be ashamed, but shall speak with their enemies in the gate."

<u>Verse 1</u>: How many of us are living in a house that we labored day and night for, that we put so much money, time, and effort into, not knowing that since we left the LORD out of our plans; no matter how big, or how beautiful it is, or how great we might feel for accomplishing it; our house is still in vain?

And how many cities, even with their armed forces, are still filled with violence and destruction? Our borders also, are still being invaded. And despite the security guards with their ready-to-attack dogs, one might hire to safeguard his property; there is still much theft, and defacement taking place. So, indeed the mere watchman is losing sleep for nothing!

Verse 2: How many of us, rather than be jobless, get up in the wee hours, to get ready to go to work; or never went to bed, because we had to work the graveyard shift, or a double shift; or stayed up all night, simply to watch our favorite TV shows?

Or, how many of us, perhaps, go to bed at night, and, instead of relaxing and going to sleep, we are tossing and turning, inhaling and exhaling, worrying about where the next dollar is coming from to pay the bills; or to buy a meal to even survive tomorrow (Matthew 6:25–34)?

Or, as opposed to looking up to God, who is beyond the ceiling, and believing that "The-LORD-Will-Provide" (Genesis 22:14), we are just lying there, staring solely at its structure, or at how damaged it is.

Verses 3 and 4: Although the fruit of our womb is an inheritance from the LORD, a blessing; how many of us have rejected God's family plan (1 Corinthians 7:1–9, Genesis 2:24), for our own (Proverbs 21:5)?

And how many of us, because we are still in our youth, see our children's existence as the arrows that pierced our lives? Which could cause us to place harm upon them (Matthew 18:1–6); or drive them to do what they ought not to do (Leviticus 19:29).

Verse 5: What is a quiver? A quiver is a sack that holds arrows. Another definition for quiver is spasm, a word that rhymes with orgasm, the very thing that is causing a lot of us to turn away from God's family plan with pleasure.

And the saddest thing about that is, when a woman gets pregnant out of wedlock, man calls it a mistake, but to God, each time she does, it is a sin (Romans 6:20–23, Colossians 3:5–6), and therefore, she truly ought to be *ashamed.*

And today, regrettably, too many of our young women are under the illusion that the man they are involved with is a keeper. And since they want to in any way keep that man, they latch on to him, through illegitimate pregnancy; or by any other means, forgetting "holiness" (Hebrews 12:7–11), that there could be grave consequences.

And lamentably, in some cases, that man still leaves to marry another, or perhaps, is already married to another (Luke 16:18); and who knows, maybe to couple others (Deuteronomy 21:15–17).

Young woman, if that man, however, is a keeper, then, why is he with you, according to his plans; visiting you, or shacking up with you, and having unlawful sex whenever he wants to, and not having you, according to God's family plan?

If that man is a keeper, then, why is he not of the mindset to have you join to him, as his wife (Mark 10:6–9), so that you both may have the right to each other (1 Corinthians 7:4), and then, you can have him enter in and out, whenever and however he pleases?

Through Proverbs 4:5–9, we are strongly advised to "Get wisdom! Get understanding!" Not get knocked up!

If you, same as me, have gone against God's family plan, "the principal thing" for us to do is seek God's forgiveness (Isaiah 43:25), and live now, according to His teachings, which began "from Galilee to this place" (Luke 23:5, Hebrews 12:9); our home.

As for our "heritage from the LORD," which we did not wait for the right time to receive from God, let us do our best to train them up in the way they should go, and pray daily that when they are old, they "will not depart from it" (Proverbs 22:6, 18:4) ever, in their life.

And in your training, remember, "Foolishness is bound up in the heart of a child" (Proverbs 22:15). So, "Do not withhold correction from a child, for if you beat him with a rod, he will not die. You shall beat him with a rod, and deliver his soul from hell" (Proverbs 23:13–14). For "He who spares his rod hates his son, but he who loves him disciplines him promptly" (Proverbs 13:24). "The rod and rebuke give wisdom, but a child left to himself brings shame to his mother." (Proverbs 29:15)

Can I tell you something real quick, about my mother?

When I was a young girl and I said or did something foolish, my mother would hit me, and then say, "Fool. See sense."

Or she would say, "Look at her; her fool bag burst now", which my youngest sibling could not stand to hear her say.

Well, there were times when I just wanted to make them both laugh, and I did. But you know what, if there is something such as a funny bag, in any of us; we have to open it now and then, so that those around us, and ourselves, can laugh, and not be disheartened all the time.

If in a family; no one is interested in making another laugh, regardless of distress; or not even in laughing at them self, like I do, at times, then, we all might as well rattle off noisily to *the open valley* and wait there for the prophet to say, "O dry bones, hear the word of the LORD!" (Ezekiel 37:1–14): "A merry heart does good, like medicine, but a broken spirit dries the bones" (Proverbs 17:22).

So, having a moral sense of humor is good for the soul; it keeps our bones moist, and from cracking all the time.

On a serious note; as a Christian mother, despite what other mothers might find online, and not in a clothing store, or a shoe store, or even a bookstore, but, in an electronic store, or a toy store, and think that it is the ideal gift for their child; you and I both already know that "Every good gift and every perfect gift is from above, and comes down from the Father of lights" (James 1:17), not from a world of darkness (Isaiah 5:20–21, Luke 11:35–36).

Many mothers may not realize, through the gifts they have bought for their children, have invited "their enemies in the gate" and into their homes, to be their children's playmates. And so, rather than their children learning how to "grow in the grace and knowledge of our Lord and Savior Jesus Christ" (2 Peter 3:18), they are being trained by their parents' misguided judgment to go in the way of the world (1 John 2:15–17, James 4:4–5, 2 Timothy 3:16–17).

After purchasing with their hard-earned money, or maybe not hard-earned; a doll baby with its improper fittings, and a playhouse with its furnishings, and getting them wrapped, they excitedly present them to their adorable, innocent little girls, as gifts. It's training time!

But, will they want to stop playing house, or know how to, when they are young women and are of age?

And for their delightful, harmless little boys; again, with their hard-earned money, or maybe not hard-earned; they buy toy guns, grenades, and daggers; and after getting them wrapped, as well, they are also presented to them, as gifts. When the reality of it is, in many countries, those plastic items are steel in the hands of many young men; employed to be natural-born killers in the sight of God (Psalm 14:2–6).

Another thing that is also attacking the minds of our little children, "Our little darlings", today, which some mothers also fail to recognize, and constantly do, because they think it is alright, is placing their child in front of the television set, or putting a contraption in his hand to keep him occupied (Proverbs 29:15) or just to settle him down.

And maybe they do that because they want uninterrupted time to do something important, or simply want some alone time.

But one device or the other, is powerful enough to zoom out his little mind from the foundation of "Jesus Christ" (1 Corinthians 3:9–15), right "on another man's foundation" (Romans 15:20).

The best thing any mother can do for her child, or her children, besides teaching them about the love and the knowledge of God, is spend quality time with them.

So to keep our laughter, today, mother, from becoming tears of sadness tomorrow, we must begin to train our children, immediately, how to "Walk as children of light" (Ephesians 5:8–17, 2:8–10), not how "To walk in the ways of darkness" (Proverbs 2:13–15, Isaiah 50:10). For "The wicked are estranged from the womb; they go astray as soon as they are born, speaking lies." (Psalm 58:3)

Remember, "Even a child is known by his deeds, whether what he does is pure and right" (Proverbs 20:11). So we ought not to be amused by everything our children say, or do. We must know how to separate what to laugh at (Ecclesiastes 3:4), from what we must right away correct (Proverbs 13:24), to keep what could for them, later, be a "sin leading to death" (1 John 5:16–17, Romans 6:23).

Imagine; while you are laughing hilariously at whatever it is your child has said, or done, and you then realized you should be correcting him (Isaiah 28:10), and not chuckling. How can you, all of a sudden, become serious, to now correct him (Jeremiah 4:22, Hosea 4:6)?

To your own child; just like "David" (1 Samuel 21:10– 15), you might appear to be mad.

I will admit though; oftentimes, the things our children say and do are ridiculously funny, and sometimes, our first reaction is we burst into laughter, and right in front of them. But when it is "foolishness" (Proverbs 15:14, 24:9), we truly should not be seen laughing at it.

"Whom will he teach knowledge?

And whom will he make to understand the message?

Those just weaned from milk?

Those just drawn from the breasts?" (Isaiah 28:9, Psalm 8:2).

Another noteworthy thing that we as parents ought to know is while it is important, today, for our children to receive a higher level of education; we must in no way, make them believe that, that education is more important than receiving God, through Christ Jesus His Son.

Because, if it is your prayer, mother, for your child, or for your children to inherit the kingdom of God" (1 Corinthians 15:50, Luke 9:23–26), same as it is mine, then, we must not fulfill their every wish, their every desire, their every asking, but in our training, be like Christ (Matthew 6:33, Philippians 2:5). By this, wherever they may go, we will be glad to know, not just their friends, but others, also, will "realized that they had been with Jesus." (Acts 4:13)

So let us, mother, as our children's first teacher, teach them how to, in their lives, make God "the Alpha and the Omega, the Beginning and the End, the First and the Last" (Revelation 22:13). So that they will not "be children, tossed to and fro and carried about with every wind of doctrine, by the trickery of men in the cunning craftiness of deceitful plotting". (Ephesians 4:14, Isaiah 30:1–5)

Let them learn from us and through us that "the LORD gives wisdom from His mouth come knowledge and understanding" (Proverbs 2:6). In this way, when they leave us, whether to attend college or to build a home of their own, they will do so according to God's plans (Psalm 33:11), not ours, nor their disobedient fathers (Hebrews 3:7–11), nor their own (Hebrews 3:12–15).

Remember, "Understanding is a wellspring of life to him who has it." (Proverbs 16:20–24, 18:4)

Let us be sure mother, to provide our children with it.

A Mother's Measure of Faith

*T*he Holy Bible lets us know that while God *poured out* some things; some things were given *by measure.*

"The love of God has been poured out in our hearts" (Romans 5:5), so that we may always "love one another" (John 13:34); and "the Holy Spirit" (Titus 3:5–6), so that we may remember "all things" (John 14:25–26) that Jesus Christ His Son has said to us. And I should say, "The wine of the wrath of God…is poured out" (Revelation 14:10), as well.

Other things such as "faith" (Romans 12:3), which "is the substance of things hoped for, the evidence of things not seen" (Hebrews 11:1); and "grace" (Ephesians 4:7), as "it is the gift of God" (Ephesians 2:8–9), we have received by measure.

Now although "God does not give the Spirit by measure" (John 3:34, Joel 2:28–29), "God has dealt to each one a measure of faith" (Roman 12:3), because "without faith it is impossible to please Him" (Hebrews 11:1–40). And so, the *measure of faith* any mother receives from God is solely for her to start pleasing God with, no other.

But what if, one mother receives from God, *a measure of faith* the size of "a mustard seed" (Matthew 17:20), and another mother, the size of "a large tree"? (Luke 13:18–19).

Does that mean the mother who received the greater *measure of faith* is favored by God, and therefore, she has no work to do?

No; because while one mother's *measure of faith* might be greater than that of another, "faith by itself, if it does not have works, is dead" (James 2:14–26), no matter how large the size might be.

Besides, "there is no partiality with God" (Romans 2:11), He does "not show personal favoritism" (Luke 20:21), to anyone (James 2:1–10).

If one mother, however, were to receive from God, a *measure of faith* greater than that of another mother, I believe it would be because when He initially, dealt to that mother, her *measure of faith*, she asked Him for a larger portion (Luke 17:5), knowing already, she was going to need it for her journey (Matthew 15:21–28).

And so to her, "God gave the increase" (1 Corinthians 3:5–8); a "good measure, pressed down, shaken together, and running over" (Luke 6:38), which she did not gamble with (John 19:23–24). She put it all in Jesus "the Son of the living God." Matthew 16:13–17

Mother, I sincerely ask you, in whom, or in what, have you placed the *measure of faith,* God has *dealt* to you?

Is it somewhere out there in "the world" (1 John 2:15–17), because you are *struggling in life,* as a single mother (John 14:27, 16:33)?

If it is somewhere out there, Mother, then, let me remind you of a man, who was in a far worse state than you might be in right now:

"The fool has said in his heart, "There is no God" (Psalm 14:1), and *struggled out of life,* believing that lie (Luke 6:45, Romans 14:11, Isaiah 45:23, Philippians 2:5–11). But you know what, despite his disbelief, his freethinking, he still has to come back (Revelation 20:12–15), to "give an account to Him who is ready to judge the living and the dead" (1 Peter 4:5, 2 Corinthians

5:10–11, Psalm 96:10–13). So let go of the world, or God will have to let go of you (Matthew 25:41).

Or perhaps, Mother, you placed the *measure of faith* God gave to you, in your only son, or daughter, and now, your heart is broken, because he, or she has turned away from godly wisdom (Proverbs 1:7–9, 10:17, 12:1, 15:10), to build a "friendship with the world". (James 4:4, Proverbs 31:1–5)

If that is the case, Mother, then, I say to you, you must get back your *measure of faith,* and quickly. Because even if your son is as old as "Methuselah" (Genesis 5:27), or whoever is the oldest in the Bible; you're going to need that same *measure of faith,* even if it is the size of a *mustard seed,* to stand before God for him, until he stands before God for himself, "with fear and trembling". (Philippians 2:12)

Or could it be Mother, that, you put the *measure of faith* God supplied you with, in some man you met, simply because he appeared to be a beacon of light; some ray of hope, during the hard and difficult times in your life? And now, he is in your home, not as your husband, but like some type of god, or "lord" (Genesis 18:12), to you, and your child, or your children.

If that is your cup, Mother, then, here is who could be filling it: "Satan himself transforms himself into an angel of light… his ministers also transform themselves into ministers of righteousness" (2 Corinthians 11:14–15).

So that man could very well be the devil himself, whom you have planted your *measure of faith* in, and that is why it cannot grow.

Or he could be one of Satan's agents shining his light in your home, and not an angel from above, shining the light of God (John 1:4–5).

Let us not be like those, who, in former times, "loved darkness rather than light" (John 3:19). And here is what we should know, Mother; God does not give us faith by measure because He might run out of faith. It is so that we may always give our measure back to Him, for it to be increased, again, and again, and again.

When God gets back a *mother's measure of faith,* He already know she wants her child, or her children to see that she can also move mountains (Matthew 17:19–20), not just pull up trees (Luke 17:6), and so, He will for every time increase it.

And when she is rewarded (1 Corinthians 2:9–10), it is not because of her workload (Ephesians 2:8–10, 1 Thessalonians 1:3), it is because of how her faith has grown in God.

When *a mother's measure of faith* has grown and is rooted in God, she can with confidence say to another, "You have faith, and I have works." Show me your faith without your works, and I will show you my faith by my works" James 2:18

When *a mother's measure of faith* has grown and is rooted in God (Psalms 16:1, 25:1–5), and not "in man" (Psalms 118:8–9, 146:3–10), nor herself (Psalm 49:11, Luke 14:11, 2 Timothy 3:1–5); unlike Peter, she is always "mindful of the things of God" (Mark 8:31–33), not worldly "possessions." Mark 10:17–25

When *a mother's measure of faith* has grown and is rooted in God; during no unsettling time in her life, will she try to keep her balance on the world's unstable foundation (Psalm 82:5, 2 Samuel 22:8). She will remain stable on God's foundation (1 Corinthians 3:11), a foundation that no one in this world has even an ounce of power to shake (Matthew 28:18, Hebrews 12:25–29).

And that's why Mother, we should always be rejoicing, praying, and giving thanks (1 Thessalonians 5:16–18), to *the Rock.*

No, not that rock!

God, "He is the Rock" (Deuteronomy 32:4), "the Rock of our salvation… the great King above all gods." (Psalm 95:1–7, Joel 2:27–29)

Now Mother, I sincerely pray "that the genuineness of your faith, being much more precious than gold that perishes, though it is tested by fire, may be found to praise, honor, and glory at the revelation of Jesus Christ". (1 Peter 1:7–13)

Chapter 3

Grateful Hearts

"We give You thanks, O LORD God Almighty,
The One who is and who was and is to come,
Because You have taken Your great power
And reigned." (Revelation 11:17)

"Praise the Lord! Oh, give thanks to the LORD,
For He is good! For His mercy endures forever."
(Psalm 106:1)

Our Gratitude

*"O*h, give thanks to the LORD!

Call upon His name; make known His deeds

Among the peoples!" (Psalm 105:1, Isaiah 12:4–6)

Heavenly Father, we declare to the nations that You are our

Banner, that You are our provider, our healer, and our peace.

We declare to the nations, Father, that You are a long-suffering

God, a trustworthy God, a faithful God, that Your lovingkindness

And Your tender mercies toward our dear mother, have not gone

Unnoticed by us and were not taken for granted.

When our mother in her youthful days had no interest in You;

God, You still cared for her, and for this, LORD, we say thank

You. Thank You for Your patience toward her, which made it

Possible for her to find You, and not, in the end, be lost.

In her latter years when she became very ill, and could no longer

Go on, in her strength, we knew it was You God, who carried

Her, to keep her from being found helpless, or lifeless, somewhere

In the street. O Father, also for this, we say, thank You.

And despite the critical condition that our mother was in, Father;

You did not let her die in a foreign land. You brought her back
Home, where "Your work… and Your glory" (Psalm 90:16)
Were seen, and not only by her children but also, by others.

Neither did You allow her to die in the home of our youngest sibling because
You knew Father, that would have made our mother's memory
A little more unbearable for her and her spirit a little harder to relax.
Not to mention the many negative words that perhaps would have
Come from others, only to make her feel like she had done something
Wrong and prevent her from seeing it as Your will, God.

Dear LORD, and please, forgive us; while we were
Recognizing our mother's weakness, as a parent, You, as her
Father, acknowledged her strength, and this guided her right back to
You (Isaiah 12:1–2).

Thank You, Father, for being our mother's shield and buckler;
For being her peace and her joy; for being her physician and her
Deliverer; for being her song, and her salvation.

O Father, and thank You for this *legacy*, may it serve as an inheritance
To every member of her generation (Joel 1:3), including those who
Never got to know her. For they will now come to know about her,
Through the great legacy she has left behind.

And may no one, Father, young, or old be disappointed in

My mother's legacy, since it is not a legacy of houses, cars, and lands,

Or of businesses, and money, for "*All, all*" those things are perishables

(Matthew 6:19–21); but will come to know that Your Word is not,

And can be passed on "for a thousand generations…"

(Deuteronomy 7:9–11, Exodus 20:1–17, Psalm 78:4–8)

Heavenly Father, may we, her first, and second generations no

Longer hold her accountable for what she did or did not do,

As a mother, or a grandmother, but search within ourselves to

Find why we, her children, and grandchildren did not

Acknowledge her, as the matriarch of the family.

Our Father, and our God, when others saw our mother and

Her first generation, as nothing, You claimed us, Yours

(Psalm 100:3), through the blood of Jesus Christ. For this,

LORD, from the depths of our hearts, we say, thank You.

Loving Father, we believe that every little detail, every song sung,

Every line said, and every course of action taken regarding our mother's

latter years and her death was orchestrated not by "flesh and blood"

(1 Corinthians 15:50), but purely by Your "Spirit". Zechariah 4:6

Therefore, the glory was not unto us, but unto You, God.

You have "done all things well" (Mark 7:37). And for this, again,

We say, thank You. In Jesus' awesome name. Amen and Amen.

One Father, One Blood, One Mind

*"B*less the LORD, O my soul; and all that is within me, bless His

Holy name! Bless the LORD, O my soul, and forget not all His benefits:

Who forgives all your iniquities,

Who heals all your diseases,

Who redeems your life from destruction,

Who crowns you with loving kindness and tender mercies,

Who satisfies your mouth with good things,

So that your youth is renewed like the eagle's."

(Psalm 103:1–5, Isaiah 40:28–31).

My LORD, I do not see that as just another one of Your powerful affirmations, but also, as a five-part question that I should answer.

And if I answer the five parts, separately, or altogether, as one;

It should not matter, since the answer either way, is the same.

And so, as I stand amid the fraction that is left of my mother's

First generation of fourteen, I look up to the heavens, and cry out;

The answer to both Your proclamation and us, is You, God! For although

We are all from the same womb; we are not all of the same father,

Which means, neither are we all, of the same blood.

So that we can be of one Father, one blood, and one mind, I brought

Them and myself to You. And as we humbly kneel before You, God,

With our heads bowed, and our eyes closed, our hearts and our minds

Are open, individually, to You, so that You may come in. As You pour

Out Your Spirit in us; fill us with love for You, God, and for one another

And with hope, Father, for "hope does not disappoint, because the love

Of God has been poured out into our hearts by the Holy Spirit who was

Given to us" (Romans 5:5), through Christ Jesus.

Our God, and our Father, before we arise from You, I seek Your blessings

once more, and not only for the generations of us, who are kneeling here

before You, but also for the generations of our dearly departed siblings.

It is acceptable Father, that they will not all have the same ambition, in life

but they can all take the same path to achieve their purpose. And

That path is the pathway "of God in Christ Jesus" (Philippians 3:14),

For it is my prayer that no one in any of our generations be lost.

I am aware Father, that, a number of our children are already living "sober

(1 Peter 5:8), and not drunken lives (Isaiah 5:11, 5:22), for

They walk "not in the flesh but in the Spirit, if indeed the Spirit of

God dwells in" (Romans 8:9–11) them; there are still many, who are abiding

in the pleasures of this world, and, are calling the success

Of it, the blessings of God (Isaiah 5:20–21, Romans 12:2).

Dear Father, please, help our generations to "not be deceived"

(James 1:16, Galatians 6:7–8); make them know LORD, that, "Every

Good gift and every perfect gift is from above, and comes down from

The Father of lights" (James 1:17), that, to be "prosperous, and… have

good success (Joshua 1:8), they must come to "Christ Jesus, who do not

walk according to the flesh, but according to the Spirit." Romans 8:1–8

And so, as far as the generations of our late siblings, and ours go,

Please, God, allow Your Holy Spirit to go, as well, to move in the

Life of each one; from infancy to adulthood, and from adulthood to infancy,

so that all may recognize that the gifts *from above,* encompass

The blood of Jesus Christ that can cleanse them from any and all iniquity

(Revelation 1:5–6), and a faith that can keep them trusting solely in

You, God (Colossians 2:6–7).

Our Father, and our God, we now rise on Your promise that,

Every curse, generational, or not, was by You, turned… into a blessing"

(Deuteronomy 23:5). We stand believing God that, not only have

You set us, and our generations "free" (John 8:36), but that

You have also cleansed us all from our iniquities; from all sickness.

God Almighty, we now go forth, to declare that, because of Christ

Jesus Your Son, we are all of one Father, one blood, and one mind; that our

relationship with You, God, and with one another is today, very prosperous.

We go forth to declare Father, that it was the Master of degrees, who shifted

what was meant for evil (Isaiah 54:17), in our lives, to make "all things

work together for good" (Romans 8:28), in our lives.

Father, at this very moment,we are declaring that it is You, God,

Who forgave all our iniquities,

Who healed all our diseases,

Who redeemed our life from destruction,

Who crowned us with lovingkindness and tender mercies,

Who satisfied our mouth with good things,

And now our youth is renewed like the eagle's, in Jesus' name. Amen.

Throw Out, and Replace

*"H*eavenly Father, I recognize through Christ Jesus that You are a

God, who has the power to heal; to cleanse; to raise the dead; to cast

Out demons (Matthew 10:7–8); that You are a God, who can replace the old

with the new (Psalm 51:10, Ezekiel 11:19–21); that You are "a God of truth

And without injustice; righteous and upright". (Deuteronomy 32:4)

And I believe that if through Christ Jesus, "we confess our sins,

He is faithful and just to forgive us our sins and to cleanse us from all

unrighteousness" (1 John 1:8–10, Isaiah 1:18); that He has the authority,

to throw out (John 2:13–16), *whatever* is not of You, God, so that

Your "Holy Spirit" (1 Corinthians 6:18–20) may dwell therein.

And so, Father, through Christ Jesus Your Son, I ask this of You,

Search us "O LORD" (Psalm 139:1 24), and *whatever* You find in

Any of us, that is hindering Your Holy Spirit from dwelling in us,

Or is declining our body, or is festering our relationship with You,

And with one another, please, God, throw out, and replace:

If You find ill will, or hatred, throw it out, and replace it with love.

If You find unforgiveness, throw it out, and replace it with forgiveness.

If You find dislike, throw it out, and replace it with friendship.

If You find cruelty, throw it out, and replace it with kindness.

If You find violence, throw it out, and replace it with peace.

If You find war, throw it out, and replace it with harmony.

If You find hurt, throw it out, and replace it with comfort.

If You find distrust, throw it out, and replace it with trust.

If You find envy, throw it out, and replace it with goodwill.

If You find bullying, throw it out, and replace it with solace.

If You find resentment, throw it out, and replace it with enjoyment.

If You find an obsession, throw it out, and replace it with actuality.

If You find depression, throw it out, and replace it with happiness.

If You find ingratitude, throw it out, and replace it with gratitude.

If You find doubt, throw it out, and replace it with faith.

If You find betrayal, throw it out, and replace it with loyalty.

If You find even one lie, throw it out, and replace it with the truth.

If You find instability, throw it out, and replace it with stability.

If You find infatuation, throw it out, and replace it with authenticity.

If You find infidelity, throw it out, and replace it with fidelity.

If You find fornication, throw it out, and replace it with self-control.

If You find slackness, throw it out, and replace it with thoroughness.

If You find negligence, throw it out, and replace it with care.

If You find laziness, throw it out, and replace it with enthusiasm.

If You find slumbering, throw it out, and replace it with vigilance.

If You find idleness, throw it out, and replace it with productivity.

If You find selfishness, throw it out, and replace it with selflessness.

If You find haughtiness, throw it out, and replace it with humbleness.

If You find cowardice, throw it out, and replace it with courage.

If You find redundancy, throw it out, and replace it with employment.

If You find barrenness, throw it out, and replace it with fruitfulness.

If You find idolatry, throw it out, and replace it with Your Son.

If You find poverty, throw it out, and replace it with godly wealth.

If You find inadequacy, throw it out, and replace it with adequacy.

If You find illiteracy, throw it out, and replace it with literacy.

If You find sickness, throw it out, and replace it with health.

If You find recklessness, throw it out, and replace it with cautiousness.

If You find foolishness, throw it out, and replace it with wisdom.

If You find favoritism, throw it out, and replace it with discernment.

If You find stinginess, throw it out, and replace it with generosity.

If You find impatience, throw it out, and replace it with patience.

If You find pessimism, throw it out, and replace it with optimism.

If You find division, throw it out, and replace it with togetherness.

If You find brokenness, throw it out, and replace it with wholeness.

If You find unnaturalness, throw it out, and replace it with naturalness.

If You find darkness, throw it out, and replace it with Your light.

If You find alcohol abuse, or any other kind of abuse,

Throw it out, and replace it with the intake of Your blood.

If You find a drug habit, or any other bad habit,

Throw it out, and replace it with the inhabitation of Your Word.

If You find shame, or disgrace,

Throw it out, and replace it with Your grace.

If You find negativity, throw it out, and replace it with positivity.

If You find any kind of challenge, throw it out, and

Replace it with the power of possibility.

Dear LORD, *whatever things* You find in any of us, that are not of You,
please, God, throw them out, and replace them. Replace them with

"Whatever things are true,

Whatever things are noble,

Whatever things are just,

Whatever things are pure,

Whatever things are lovely,

Whatever things are of good report…" (Philippians 4:8).

So that each one of us, Father, may have the "mind…which was also in

Christ Jesus" (Philippians 2:5) Your Son, and

Abound in love,

Abound in prayer,

Abound in faith,

"Abound in hope" (Roman 15:13, Psalm 68:19),

Abound in service, and in "joy and peace",

Through Your Holy Spirit, everlastingly.

In Jesus' mighty name. Amen and Amen.

Reflections

*H*eavenly Father, when others put their trust in the mirror;

I put my "trust in You" (Psalm 9:10), because "as for God,

His way is perfect; the word of the Lord is proven; He is a shield

To all who trust in Him." (2 Samuel 22:31)

Father, and while others spend time in the mirror (James 1:22–25),

Grooming themselves, and do not move until they are pleased with

The results, I am aware God, that You are in heaven watching me,

And will not move, either, on my behalf, unless You are pleased

With the way, in which I am living my life. (Psalm 14:2–3)

I recognize Father, "a mirror, dimly" (1 Corinthians 13:12)

Shows a man how he looks on the outside, but Your word tells him

Clearly, how he looks on the inside. (Matthew 23:25–28)

Therefore, to not be rejected by You, God (1 Samuel 16:7),

When others look in the mirror, to fix what they can see is wrong,

On the outside of them; I look in Your word, to correct what is wrong

with me, on the inside.

Because I already know the mirror breaks; "The grass withers,

The flower fades, but the word of God stands forever" (Isaiah 40:8);
And must abide daily, in me (John 15:7), so that I may through
Your Son, "have everlasting life." (John 3:16)

When others look in the mirror, Father, and can see their own
Reflection; I see the reflection of the one, who has been with me
From inception, and every other stage of my life. O LORD and
I rejoice because our umbilical cords are still beautifully intertwined, even
to this very day.

When others look in the mirror, Father, and can see their own
Reflection, I see the reflection of the one who cried with me
Through every heartache and pain. I see the reflection of the one
Who reminds me that, if I continue to trust in You, God, and Your
Holy Word, any tears I shed in sadness, will sooner than I know,
Become tears of joy. (Psalm 30:5)

When others look in the mirror, Father, and can see their own
Reflection, I see the reflection of the one, who, when I slip,
Catches me, not come tripping behind me, because she knows
I must have been "drunk with wine" (Ephesians 5:17–18),
To have stumbled away from Your holy Word.

When others look in the mirror, Father, and can see their own
Reflection, I see the reflection of the one, whom I know,

If I do not live right, could become a case of mistaken identity

By my wrongdoings in life.

When others look in the mirror, Father, and can see their own

Reflection, I see the reflection of the one, whom I know, will love me; will

laugh with me; and caringly at me; and will in Your truth, stand

By me, and, for me, until You draw her spirit, or mine, back to

You, God. (Ecclesiastes 12:7)

Dear LORD, and if You draw my spirit before hers, when You are

Comforting her, please, let her know that, I have before now, asked

You to give her the strength to carry on without me, for the sake of

Her own soul, and for this ministry.

Yet, I pray, LORD, that You will not withdraw her spirit, nor mine,

Any time soon. Instead, since this is just the beginning of our ministry

For You, God, may You, by Your grace, and by Your mercy,

Grant us both longevity of life (Philippians 1:6).

Heavenly Father, O LORD, my God, when I see a dark cloud that

Shows off its silver lining, for it represents hope, I am glad.

Father, when I see "the appearance of a rainbow in a cloud on a rainy day…

the appearance of the brightness all around it… the appearance

Of the likeness of the glory of the LORD" (Ezekiel 1:28), I am glad.

Father, when I see the satiny moon, accompanied by a host of

Shining stars that You have made to give light on the earth, I am glad.

Father, when I see the enchanting trees that make a lovely arc over a pathway;
knowing it is the beauty of Your handiwork, I am glad.

Father, when I hear the birds chirping loudly and sweetly, before the break
of dawn; alerting me that it is time to have worship, I am glad.

Heavenly Father, when I see the splendor and the radiance that exist from
the things, which You have "given to all the peoples under the whole heaven
as a heritage" (Deuteronomy 4:19), I am glad.

O Father, can I tell You, when I see how You have allowed another,

To be identical to me, and not only in features, and gender, but also in
mind, and spirit, I am glad, and like the silver lining, I show off too.

I show off Father, because, when I reflect on her poise, her beauty, outwardly,
and more so, inwardly (1 Peter 3:4); when I think of her kindness, her love,
and the joy and laughter she has brought to my life; when I see her there
for me, not only as a sister but also as my best Friend, I know God, she
exists with all these wonderful attributes,

Because then, You were thinking only of me.

Through her, Father, You have shown me, in life, "Two are better

Than one, because they have a good reward for their labor. For if they

Fall, one will lift up his companion. But woe to him who is alone

When he falls, for he has no one to help him up" (Ecclesiastes 4:9–10), and

even "Though one may be overpowered by another, two can withstand

him. And a threefold cord is not quickly broken"

(Ecclesiastes 4:12), unless, God, it is broken by You.

That is why when our threefold cord became a twofold cord,

I knew it was You, God, who did that. Therefore, I have no regrets,

About not getting to know our brother (Job 14:1–2), since only

You know if he would have turned out to be a wise man, or a

Foolish man (Ecclesiastes 10:2, Proverbs 4:23). Only You know

God, what evil can come "out of the heart of men" (Mark 7:21–23),

Even before it could be made known (Proverbs 27:19).

Father, words are not enough, to express to You, how grateful I am,

For the one, and to the one, whom You have left to labor with me.

But O Father, when I search my own life, I see that I have nothing

As valuable as You have, to give her, in return.

So, here I am, LORD, not in the mirror, but solely before You, God,

And not with the same old repetitive prayer that I usually come to You with

for myself. I came to You, this time, with the heart's agenda of

The one, whom You have given to me. For I know LORD, You have

The power to search it (Psalm 139:1–24), and to rearrange it, if need be.

O LORD, and if You find that You have to shift it around; or

Add something to it; or scratch off a thing, or two, that's all right.

Make any arrangement You have to; Father, even if You have to

Create a whole new agenda, Yourself, then, go right ahead,

And do whatever You have to, for I trust fully in You.

Heavenly Father, and now I thank You for the large bouquet of

Beautiful promises that You have placed in the heart of my

Beloved sister and best friend forever.

As she continues to tread this life's pathway, as she journeys on,

May she always be sheltered and protected by You, God. May Your grace, and Your goodness shine forth radiantly each day, from her, and not only in her home, but also on her job, and on all others whom she meets, or who meet her. And may her eyes Father, never look down; let them always be lifted to You, God (Psalm 121), for by this her spirit will remain only in You. In the mighty name of Jesus Christ Your Son. Amen and Amen.

Chapter 4

The Conclusion

"**W**hat is the conclusion then?"
(1 Corinthians 14:15)
"The end of a thing is better than its beginning".
(Ecclesiastes 7:8)

The Front Cover

On the front cover of this book, I wanted to display something
that can identify with the womb of a woman, and I thought the ideal
thing would be a flower.

Because the same as a woman's "gentle and quiet spirit"
(1 Peter 3:3–4) gets the attention of God, a beautiful and unique
flower captures the attention of a woman.

And while searching for a flower, this little one, which is shown
Much larger than its actual size, trumpeted off louder than all the
Others; even the big ones, and got my full attention.

After examining it very closely; although it is our National Flower,
I only realized then its distinctiveness, and I could not help
but make it my choice for the front cover of 'The Fruit of the Womb.'

Now, if something else, other than the front cover, got you
Interested in reading this book, then, I hope, that when you
Have read 'A Portrait of the Yellow Elder', it brings you

To recognize the powerful, and brilliant work of God,

Divinely proclaimed through the Yellow Elder. A small

Golden flower, that perhaps, are not recognized by a

lot of us, despite it being our National Flower.

And if you still, then, do not find the description of this flower,

that was designed by God, same as the woman's womb, as striking

as I do, well, I hope then, at least one thing, within the covers of

This book brings you to understanding something new about God,

And also to accepting His truth, through Jesus Christ our Lord.

<h1 style="text-align:center">A Portrait of the Yellow Elder</h1>

While the Yellow Elder is a very small flower, the tree itself can Grow tall and spread wide; directing us to *look up to the hills.*

Its brightness is the reflection of the glory of God, shining down on our Bahama-land; on our archipelago of islands.

The stripes in the corolla are there to remind us of the ones, Jesus painfully and willingly took; proclaiming by *His stripes we are healed.*

The red represents the blood, that from His *wounded* and *bruised* body, Dripped expressively onto the ground.

The soft velvety texture of the petals signifies that the Holy Spirit is

At work, daily, in the life of everyone who believes in the Son of God.

And same as these three: the Yellow Elder, yellow bells and yellow trumpet bush are one, so is God the Father, the Son, and the Holy Spirit.

The bell shape symbolizes the trumpet of God that will sound, as *The Lord Himself will descend from heaven with a shout"*.

The clusters illustrate the *remnant of every nation, tribe, tongue, and people–* going 'Forward, Upward, Onward Together' *to meet the Lord in the air, and thus we shall always be with the Lord.*

Scriptures to Reflect on:

Psalm 121:1–2, Isaiah 53:1–12, Luke 23:26–49, John 3:1–21, Romans 8:1–11, 8:31–39, 9:27, 1 Thessalonians 4:13–18, Hebrews 10:11–18, 1 John 5:6–13, Revelation 14:6, 22:12–21

The Woman, the Womb, and the Flower

A woman is like the petals of a flower; beautiful, sweet, soft, and delicate.

And same as the life of a flower begins with a seed, and has an ovary; a Woman's womb has ovaries, and conception therein, also, begins with a seed.

As a flower receives nutrients through its stem; the woman, through The umbilical cord, gives nutrients and oxygen to her baby.

And just as the bud of a flower goes from stage to stage, enlarges,

And opens into maturity; the fetus also, goes from stage to stage

And then, head down, causing the woman to expand for delivery.

"A woman, when in labor, has sorrow because her hour has come;

But as soon as she has given birth to the child, she no longer remembers

The anguish, for joy that a human being has been born into the world."

(John 16:21)

A flower, when it is seasonal, the florist has to wait for it to be in season, and

When it is in season and is in her possession, she forgets how long she

Had been waiting for it, because when she sees it, she remembers its

Beauty is unlike any other, in this world.

A Mother's Journal of Faith

A Mother's Journal of Faith

A Mother's Journal of Faith

A Mother's Journal of Faith

A Mother's Journal of Faith

A Mother's Journal of Faith

A Mother's Journal of Faith

A Mother's Journal of Faith

A Mother's Journal of Faith

A Mother's Journal of Faith

A Mother's Journal of Faith

A Mother's Journal of Faith

A Mother's Journal of Faith

A Mother's Journal of Faith

A Mother's Journal of Faith

A Mother's Journal of Faith

A Mother's Journal of Faith

A Mother's Journal of Faith

A Mother's Journal of Faith

A Mother's Journal of Faith

A Mother's Journal of Faith

A Mother's Journal of Faith

A Mother's Journal of Faith

A Mother's Journal of Faith

A Mother's Journal of Faith

A Mother's Journal of Faith

A Mother's Journal of Faith

A Mother's Journal of Faith

A Mother's Journal of Faith

A Mother's Journal of Faith

A Mother's Journal of Faith

A Mother's Journal of Faith

A Mother's Journal of Faith

A Mother's Journal of Faith

A Mother's Journal of Faith

A Mother's Journal of Faith

A Mother's Journal of Faith

A Mother's Journal of Faith

A Mother's Journal of Faith

A Mother's Journal of Faith

A Mother's Journal of Faith

A Mother's Journal of Faith

A Mother's Journal of Faith

A Mother's Journal of Faith

A Mother's Journal of Faith

A Mother's Journal of Faith

A Mother's Journal of Faith

A Mother's Journal of Faith

A Mother's Journal of Faith

A Mother's Journal of Faith

A Mother's Journal of Faith

A Mother's Journal of Faith

A Mother's Journal of Faith

A Mother's Journal of Faith

A Mother's Journal of Faith

A Mother's Journal of Faith

A Mother's Journal of Faith

A Mother's Journal of Faith

A Mother's Journal of Faith

A Mother's Journal of Faith

A Mother's Journal of Faith

A Mother's Journal of Faith